MW00459471

The Modern Trader

Wall Street Traders Reveal Their Formula for Success

T3Live

Sean Hendelman, CEO & Scott Redler, CSO

Marketplace Books

Publisher: Chris Myers
VP/General Manager: John Boyer
Senior Editor: Courtney Jenkins
Editorial Coordinator: Danielle Hainsey
Editorial Intern: Andrea Racine
Art Director/Designer: Larry Strauss
Graphic Designer: Jennifer Marin
Production Design Interns: Jessica Weedlun & Morgan DiPietro

ISBN 10: 1-59280-449-7
ISBN 13: 978-1-59280-449-8
Printed in the United States of America.

 **T3LIVE.COM**

As Featured By:

The Wall Street Journal

Investor's Business Daily

The New York Times

Active Trader Magazine

TRADERS Magazine

Advanced Trading Magazine

New York Post

CNBC TV and CNBC.com

Bloomberg Television

Forbes.com

Fox Business News

TheStreet.com

Minyanville

and Senator Ted Kaufman,
on the floor of the United States Senate

Contents

Foreword

IIIIIIIIIIIIIIIIIIIIIIIIIIIIIIIIII

From the Editor

I JUMPED ON THE 4 TRAIN IN MANHATTAN, HEADING downtown for the first day of my internship with T3, not knowing what to expect. I had just completed my junior year of college and I was pleased to have landed a gig with one of the most respected trading firms on the street. After seeing T3 traders appear on CNBC with increasing regularity, I found myself eating dinner and drinking wine with these highly-respected market technicians on my first night that summer in New York. In between bites of steak at Bobby Van's on Broad Street, they talked about trading and what to expect from my summer. Their enthusiasm was impossible to overlook. They each loved their job. After a few glasses of wine and one trip in the wrong direction on the subway, I managed to make it home to my dorm for the summer in the Gramercy section of Manhattan. Lying in bed, hoping I would not oversleep and arrive late on my second day of work, I could not help but look forward to what the summer had in store.

The stock market had always interested me, and I was looking forward to learning more about trading. Still, I had no idea that I had just walked into a firm on the cusp of something special. The market was especially active as volatility ramped up ahead of the economic tsunami that would soon drench Americans with paralyzing fear.

Before that summer, I knew little about active stock trading. During that summer, I learned more than I could have ever imagined. After that summer, I knew it would be hard for me to bring myself to go into any other career. Trading is a truly special adventure.

As my internship wore on, I understood more and more what made the partners at T3 tick. I learned the improbable and inspiring stories about how they became traders and ended up joining forces to create this one-of-a-kind company. I gleaned lessons learned from their journeys into trading. The inevitable realization I had is one other traders surely experienced many times before me—there is no business like trading and even more so, there is no business like your *own* business.

I wanted to learn as much as possible in my time at T3 because I could sense the rare opportunity I had been given having come into this firm at this time. There were no guarantees I would ever have such an opportunity again. The partners were in the process of planning a book about trading, telling their stories and teaching the T3 way. They hoped to tell their stories and inspire others to get the most out of their trading careers or investing activities. Late in the summer, we all came to the realization that I was in a unique position to tell their story.

While most of the financial community was battered in the global credit crisis and subsequent market collapse, prepared traders were able to weather the storm and come out stronger on the other side. As the market went bust, educated traders were prepared with what the stock charts had been telling them for months: the system was broken.

A team of young guys from diverse backgrounds had come together to have their best year ever during the greatest financial crisis of their generation. In trading, you must learn something new every day. Those who do not remain fluid are left behind, and those who adapt become that much stronger. The T3 team taught me more than any college student could ever hope to learn in a summer, and I hope you learn as much from their stories as I have.

John Darsie
Business Editor, T3 Live

Preface

Live from Wall Street: What to Expect

W ALL STREET CAN BE A LONELY PLACE. FINANCE is a highly competitive industry, a dog-eat-dog world. Competition in trading can be cutthroat. Older traders tell stories of failed partnerships, where others were more interested in taking advantage of them than working together to move forward. Many traders are greedy individuals who join the trading ranks in the hope of riding the latest get-rich-quick wave.

But now, a community has been created with the freedom of an electronic, more transparent stock market, where anyone can access a sea of information and have the opportunity to be a profitable trader. Through professional analysis and collaboration, traders can maximize their abilities and continue to grow every day.

The desire to help others achieve trading success is what makes Sean prod others to be productive, keeps Marc at his trading desk long hours, gets Scott up early each morning, compels Evan to plaster charts all over his wall, and obliges Nadav to sacrifice his own trading to teach others the craft. The partners of T3 Live want to help others escape the corporate struggle that consumed them and feel the hope and freedom that comes with becoming an entrepreneur.

All five partners started trading careers as pure novices with no real knowledge of what it would take to become successful traders. In Part I of this book, you will hear the stories of how each partner became a trader, and what each learned along the way. The paths that lead to the amazing world of trading are largely different. Traders come from all walks of life, because in this industry, temperament and discipline are more important components of success than any other factor.

Hopefully the stories will inspire you to—at the very least— educate yourself about active investing. The ultimate goal of this book is to equip you with powerful tools to conquer the market. By teaching through the context of the last recession, one that was unique in the history of the market, these lessons are more interesting and relevant. The ability to dictate your own success in a competitive, high-energy environment makes trading a one-of-a-kind business. With a lot of hard work, optimism, and discipline, you can achieve success on your own terms.

"Do not go where the path may lead, go instead where there is no path and leave a trail."

-Ralph Waldo Emerson

The Modern Trader

1

Financial Crises Past and Present

I N THE LAST 20 YEARS, THERE HAVE BEEN THREE KEY times in the market when everyone wanted to be involved in the action. During these periods, the markets dominated the headlines. Talk of the mind-boggling returns ruled happy hour conversations. Traders lived the job. Long hours were spent at the trading desk. When traders left the office, the market did not leave them. There would be no vacations, not during times likes these. With all the money out there to be made, everyone made sure they came into the office focused and ready. Every day, something new happened to increase volatility and expand opportunity. In exciting times, many rush into the market, thinking they too can make a fortune. The ones who make the real money, not just off the tip of the iceberg, during these times are the ones who have been there all along. Times like these make you realize the foolishness of putting money into a fund that is not actively managed, or into a retirement account that is subject to the irresponsible behavior of others. But most of all, these times prove why it is great to be an active trader.

THE ASIAN CONTAGION

The first such period began in July 1997. "The Asian Contagion," as it was dubbed, raised very real fears of a global financial meltdown. "Contagion" refers to the idea of a crisis rapidly spreading because of the interconnectedness of the global economy. Deep-rooted problems gradually sweep the globe from one neighboring country to another.

This particular crisis began in Thailand after the government there decided to remove the country's currency peg from the dollar. The country experienced tremendous growth in GDP as the government spent lavishly to build record-setting skyscrapers. The problem was that while jobs and spending were growing, there was no demand to match. All Asian currencies were greatly devalued and the markets crashed. Hedge funds on the wrong side of the action imploded, causing further pain and volatility in the market. Thailand had acquired so much foreign debt by trying to live beyond its means that the country went bankrupt well before the currency collapse. This may sound eerily familiar to another financial crisis, but we will get to that later. During this period of crashing markets and raging stocks, senior traders led firms while a new crop of traders was being harvested, many of the top traders at T3 included.

DOT-COM BOOM

The dot-com period of market frenzy was different in nature from the Asian Contagion and the 2008 financial crisis because the craze was not the result of panic, but of raging bullishness. By all accounts, monkeys could have made money trading during the dot-com boom. The profits were ridiculous, and in the end, proved to be unsustainable. For traders, it was great while it lasted.

Prefix and suffix investing—buying anything with an "e" or ".com" attached to it—was the genius strategy that made the boldest investors instant millionaires. The rise of the Internet was akin to the invention of the automobile; it completely changed the way we live. The World Wide Web created a brand new world of endless possibilities, and overexcitement created a massive bubble. New technology companies focused on capturing market share rather than making profits, but nobody seemed to care. Rather than focusing on reasonable valuations, investors bought highly-touted IPOs and stocks with the greatest upward momentum, hoping the madness would continue. Inevitably, the market eventually came crashing down.

The opportunists were swept out of the industry, and what remained was a group of savvy and sophisticated true professionals. For more than eight years following the end of the dot-com era, the market stagnated in a lull. There was movement, but lower volume made trading more difficult. Money was out there to be made, but each dollar had to be earned. History, we have learned, is bound to repeat itself in some form. The next bubble was already being inflated. Traders knew it was only a matter of time before volatility spiked and opportunity returned.

CRISIS OF CREDIT

Finally, we come to the financial credit crisis of the late 2000s.

The American Dream represents the opportunity for anyone, no matter race, religion, or background, to prosper while living a free and happy life. It is what makes our country unique and inspires our success as a society. Sadly, the American Dream has become distorted.

The sub-prime mortgage crisis illustrates how companies and individuals got carried away with trying to live beyond their means. Mortgage companies exploited those eager to own a home by offering adjustable rate mortgages people would not be able to pay. Interest rates spiked in the second and third year of these mortgages, forcing people out of their homes and flooding the market with foreclosures. Rather than work to keep people in their homes, companies opted to try and sell these vacated homes at bargain basement prices. The housing market flooded with cheap foreclosed homes and property values plummeted.

While the actions of mortgage lenders were deplorable, the most explosive and damaging part of this crisis came from Wall Street, where investment banks constructed new derivatives and further leveraged assets. Banks saw mortgage-backed securities as a new opportunity to dupe investors. The problem was that many of these securitized mortgages were sub-prime, predatory loans, rendering many of the investments completely worthless. And the rating agencies were ignorant to the inherent danger of these assets.

Bear Stearns Failure

The people at Bear Stearns knew the assets were worthless, but they leveraged them anyway, more than 30 times over in some cases. Investment banks showed a complete disregard for the American public, often betting against the very investments they sold to state pension funds and insurance companies. As investor losses mounted in asset-backed securities investments—a concept, along with securitization, that they pioneered—the company increased its exposure to the mortgage-backed assets that were central to the subprime crisis. Many had forecast the potential disaster that would ensue when the real estate bubble burst, but greedy executives did not care because the bonuses were still rolling in.

Hedge funds with the most exposure to sub-prime risk imploded, including several mammoth funds at Bear Stearns. The prime brokerage unit that was considered the best in the industry oversaw the greatest number of hedge fund failures in history. Clients withdrew capital from accounts as all confidence was lost, and over the course of a few days, the bank became insolvent. Not even an emergency loan from the Federal Reserve could restore confidence and save the company. In a distress sale, Bear Stearns—with a 52-week high share price of $133.20—was sold to JP Morgan for $10 per share, a coup considering the initial agreed-upon price of $2 per share. At that price, the value of the company's office complexes would have almost exceeded its sale price. With the bottomless pit that was Bear's debt obligations, it is no wonder it had to basically be given away.

A company that was worth hundreds of billions of dollars one day was suddenly broke the next. The idea was scary in and of itself. No one imagined anything like this could ever happen in our banking system. Now, anything seems possible. With the interconnectedness of the modern world financial system, the first domino had fallen in what would be a thunderous collapse.

Bear Stearns, although highly regarded, entered into a large amount of risky investments, and most fund managers were aware of that fact. Although lack of proper regulation made credit default swaps and collateralized debt obligations (CDOs) legal instruments, there is no doubt that many practices were highly unethical. Still, most thought the company's failure would be an isolated incident. As it turned out, Bear Stearns' irresponsible behavior was only a symptom of the disease that would bring the financial system and world economy to their knees.

The fear during those months following the collapse of Bear Stearns was palpable. During the Asian Contagion, the gravest problems existed many thousands of miles away. During the dot-com boom, people got burned for being greedy. This time it was different. This time, the entire engine of our economy was failing. Lending was almost halted. Without a flow of capital, existing small businesses died out while new ones could never form. Taxpayers lost savings in failing regional banks and saw pensions evaporate.

Lehman Brothers Failure
The outlook was bleak and continued to worsen as Lehman Brothers was forced to liquidate its assets in a Chapter 11

bankruptcy filing. A true icon in the industry, Lehman's collapse was a painful indication that the worst was yet to come. The company once operated from three floors of the World Trade Center, and while only a single employee was lost in the September 11 attacks, those and other nearby offices were rendered unusable by the debris from the towers' collapse. The company rallied, setting up a makeshift trading floor in Jersey City before eventually purchasing a new building in midtown Manhattan from rival Morgan Stanley. Lehman Brothers had become a symbol of hope for post 9/11 New York as employees went back to work.

The company's failure, and the same employees' departure from that midtown office on September 15, 2008, was likewise an iconic moment and symbolic of the times. Images of employees streaming out of the building with items bearing company logos became headline fodder, reinforcing just how dire a state the financial system was in. The problem was clearly systemic, and there was no end in sight. What would be the next domino to fall? The government-sponsored takeovers that prevented the whole house from coming down.

The financial world was already in turmoil when the summer of 2008 rolled around. With one scandal after another destroying what was left of the public's trust in Wall Street, bankers looked for yet another way to make a credible investment into their own personal casinos. While investors were now scared of anything that resembled a derivative, Wall Street made the physical commodities market its new pet. Energy commodities, especially oil, became the new hottest thing in town. As the dollar was falling and the real estate market imploded, investor flight to commodities ensured that the new project was off and running. While commodity futures were originally created for growers and producers to hedge against sudden price drops, they had now become another vehicle for speculation. The price of a single barrel of oil went from $60 in the middle of 2007 to as high as $147 during the summer of 2008. The inexplicable rise in crude prices sent the prices at the pump skyrocketing to record levels of more than $4 per gallon in the United States. By 2008, a barrel of oil was traded an average of 27 times before it was actually consumed. The sudden rise in gas prices only served to increase the hysteria that gripped American society.

Volatility rose to unprecedented levels. Consumer confidence fell to near all-time lows. Impossible decisions had to be made, and they were. In a perfect world, government would be small, regulation would be minimal, and taxes would be low. But we do not live in a perfect world. The damage would have been catastrophic had the entire system been allowed to fail. Another great depression seemed a not-so-remote possibility. The government stepped in to cushion the fall. New regulation is being put in place to prevent abuses by corporations, and plans are being made to reshape our energy future in a way that should provide a lasting boost to the economy and national security. The only missing piece going forward will be a more responsible public.

PREPAREDNESS, ACCOUNTABILITY, AND CONTROL

The Asian Contagion, the dot-com boom, and the credit crisis were all explosive in their own way. Each caused a lot of pain for a lot of people. The world, and the market, is cyclical. There are periods of calm followed by periods of high volatility. Just when you think lessons have been learned, another bubble is created and another crisis is born. The fact of the matter is, there will always be those greedy individuals and companies who push the envelope too far, and the unwitting public will always become fearful when things hit the fan. Given the unpredictable nature of the cycle, it is foolish not to maintain a degree of control over your financial future.

Active trading gives you the chance to seize control and be confident that your money is safe no matter what is going on around you. As investors during the 2008 market meltdown can attest, having no control when the market is tanking is one of the most helpless feelings imaginable. Do not let yourself be at the mercy of the system. Educate yourself with the help of real professional traders who are in the trenches every day. If you live a mantra of preparedness and account-ability, you will save yourself a great deal of pain, and even profit during the times when others are suffering. History will repeat itself in some form, but if we are ready to face the challenges ahead, we will prosper. Active trading allows individuals to be prepared for any market or economy. We do not have to subject ourselves to the fate of the masses. Through active trading, equip yourself with the tools to be successful and empower yourself to control your own destiny.

• • •

2

How T3 Came to Be

THE DAY THE FIVE PARTNERS MET, FIVE TRADERS agreed to join forces. Before the encounter, they all figured it would be just another meeting, similar to ones they often took, looking for opportunities to advance their businesses. It was a thirst for growth that made each of them highly successful entrepreneurs. Introduced through acquaintances who identified a mutual eagerness for expansion, Sean Hendelman, Marc Sperling, Scott Redler, Nadav Sapeika, and Evan Lazarus immediately struck a chord. Each had no pre-conceived notion as to what qualities the others would offer and no expectation that a deal would be struck at any point. All had been involved in several trading partnerships, and each required a long feeling-out process before any deal could be reached.

AT FIRST MEETING

In this instance, the fit was perfect. Usually, it takes time to identify how someone's strength will mesh with another's. At the time of this first meeting, Sean Hendelman and Nadav Sapeika were partners at Nexis, a trading firm with a very strong training program and many skilled young traders, as well as an extensive blackbox trading business. Marc Sperling, Scott Redler, and Evan Lazarus were the partners at Sperling Enterprises, a trading firm with many older traders who were some of the heaviest hitters on the Street. Each firm had a core competency that drove its consistent success, but neither had the full package. Something was missing.

At Nexis, Sean and Nadav had worked tirelessly to develop the highly successful training program that boasted a much higher than average industry retention rate for new traders. In a business where only close to ten percent survive more than a year, close to half of the traders under their tutelage reached profitability. The program was thorough, but only incorporated a narrow school of shorter term scalp trading. More content and credibility was needed to take it to the next level. They dreamed of a comprehensive training program backed by a well-established trading firm. Sperling Enterprises was the perfect match.

The synergy between the two organizations was apparent from day one, and it was easy for all parties to come to an agreement later that same day. After achieving consistent success training new traders, Nadav and Sean sought a way to channel the program into something that could be made available to a broader audience. The trading floor is a unique and exciting environment. The most successful firms foster a sense of teamwork and camaraderie that facilitates good, disciplined training. Traders work together, sharing stocks in play, noting ones that are at important levels and calling out those making moves. Veterans mentor young traders. Everyone shares analysis and ideas, making information available for eager traders to learn and improve their skills.

While the internet has created a whole new platform for people around the world to interact through social networking, the trading world had yet to sufficiently incorporate the web. With an increasing ability to communicate, trading could become an even more transparent and inclusive venture. Everyone involved recognized the opportunity to leverage the new powerhouse trading firm into a one-of-a-kind, first-of-its-type community of traders.

T3 Live was born. Today, traders all over the world plug into the T3 Virtual Trading Floor to watch live videos, read extensive analysis, and listen to top traders throughout each trading day. Traders new to the business tune in to the complete school of training courses to first build a foundation for trading, while a broader range of traders enroll in advanced courses to sharpen their trading tools. T3 Live continues to grow into a hub for trading, and with each passing day, its value grows with the swelling ranks of traders.

Never in their years of trading had any of the founding partners of T3 ever struck a deal within a month of meeting eventual partners, and in a single day, they created T3 together. The allure of the T3 Live concept was at the time too exciting to wait. As keen as Marc, Sean, Scott, Nadav, and Evan were to join forces that day, it still would have been hard to believe how well the merger would work out, and how close they are to their dream today.

THE TRADERS

The strength of T3 Live exists in the unique qualities that make each partner successful. There is very little overlap in the core competencies of each partner, and it is impossible to say one is more important than the next, because without any one individual, the group's strength would be infinitely less.

SEAN

Sean is the invisible hand that guides the business and directs the vision for each T3 project. A facilitator by nature, he works in the background, pulling strings and challenging others to make the most of their skills. His ambition is contagious. Sean's passion for entrepreneurship and desire to blaze his own trail inspire others around him to take the mantle. The same spirit that fueled his success at a third grade bake sale makes T3 Live a leader in the world of trading education. The same zest for growth propelled him up the corporate ladder at Greenwich Capital Markets before he heeded the call of entrepreneurship.

At T3, Sean has found an ideal venue to apply his entrepreneurial skills. While individual traders get acclaim for large profits, his blackbox trading systems often generate more profits in a single day than the entire firm combined. Each step of his journey in trading taught a valuable lesson that led to where he is today. Although the blackboxes are a large part of the firm, Sean's greatest contribution is as a leader. He knows where we are, where we want to go, and what we need to do to get there. The enthusiasm of his vision drives the firm forward.

MARC

Marc is the natural. A highly profitable trader since before the dot-com boom, Marc has proven his ability to adapt to the constant changes. He manages many positions at a time, using sharp instincts to identify chart patterns and intuition to enter and exit trades. Watching Marc trade is like watching a great pitcher work a hitter; great results are achieved with the ease only seen in someone with undeniable natural ability. He is passionate about what he does, and finds it difficult to understand why everyone does not share his appetite for action.

During the summer of 2009, as the rest of the partners headed out to play golf at a charity outing, Marc reluctantly tagged along. He loves playing golf, but after the capitulation of housing lenders Fannie Mae and Freddie Mac, there was increased volatility during the usually quiet summer months. With such money-making opportunities out there, Marc found it almost impossible to leave his trading station.

Marc's sheer ability allows him to squeeze profits out of any market, and the T3 Live team has worked hard to channel his genius into a vital part of its training program.

SCOTT

Scott is the workhorse, and the face of T3 Live. Scott takes a highly disciplined approach to everything he does. The first one into the office every day by a long shot, he prepares materials to guide all of our subscribers. He shoots the in-depth market analysis videos that provide invaluable information each morning and every afternoon. Scott has an iron will to succeed in trading and everything he does.

After the passing of his best friend, Steven Perez, who died at age 29 just weeks after being diagnosed with Leukemia, Scott devoted himself to getting the most out of his able body. He has competed in more than 20 triathlons and one Ironman competition, the most grueling test in all of sport, to raise money for the Steven M. Perez Foundation. Many

T3 VIDEO 🎥 ·······································
Search "CNBC Scott Redler" on T3Live.com's YouTube page to see Scott's most notable appearances.

days during lunch, Scott can be found at the gym, swimming laps and riding the bike. While others head off to the beach after work on Friday, Scott is often headed to an intense triathlon training camp for the weekend.

"The Red Dog," as he is nicknamed, shows this same level of dedication to his trading. Scott knows the market inside and out. He has made more than 100 appearances on CNBC, with each one coming more quickly after another as hosts embrace his quick-witted analysis and enthusiasm. A great trader, his passion and drive go beyond just his career. Scott is prepared for every hour of every day of his life. His commitment to preparation makes T3 Live possible; his knowledge and charisma are what make it special.

EVAN

Evan is the guru; he oozes with passion for the market. Evan is always looking at charts and knows what he does well. The strongest technician at the firm, he never stops thinking about patterns. Every day, Evan comes in early and stays late to analyze charts and identify technical patterns. He provides a great example for young traders, as he had to work hard to develop his own trading. Evan worked his tail off to get where he is today and continues to grow as a trader. A gifted teacher, he understands the psychology of trading as well as anyone. Evan makes himself available to any trader who has questions or needs mentoring. His technical expertise makes his favorite chart setups trades to watch each morning.

NADAV

Nadav has trained hundreds of traders over the course of his career.

His optimism radiates throughout the office; his jokes keep the trading floor light and often full of laughter. This positive approach to life allowed him to persevere after he moved alone to the United States from South Africa at 17. Working as a waiter at night for several years to pay for his living expenses while trading during the day, Nadav did what it took to make a career for himself in trading. His approach to teaching is fun, and there is a method to everything he does. Nadav's lessons in trading are injected with hilarious anecdotes and metaphors. Traders cannot be carried across the finish line, but he makes sure they have every opportunity to make it to the promised land as a trader.

STORIES & LESSONS

Each partner started his professional career in more conventional settings, working long hours with little satisfaction or reward. After catching a glimpse of what trading offers, each jumped at the chance to achieve success on his own terms. The leap created a great deal of fear and uncertainty because nobody is guaranteed success in trading—far from it. Consistent success as a trader remains difficult to achieve, but if unnecessary risks are avoided and the proper education is undertaken, odds of success greatly increase and the chance for painful losses dissipates. Hopefully, each of the partners' stories will inspire others to have the confidence to take control and become an active trader, and the lessons they have learned along the way can guide new traders to success.

• • •

Part I
||||||||||||||||||||||

Stories

3

Sean Hendelman
The Patriarch

ANSWERING THE CALL

A CALL FROM MY BEST FRIEND IN 1999 CHANGED MY LIFE FOREVER.

"I made $300,000 trading stocks today!" he boasted. The idea of trading had always interested me, and with people making hundreds of thousands of dollars in a single day, I was all ears.

The call came at a seemingly inopportune time. I had just been promoted to vice president at Greenwich Capital Markets. I had received the biggest bonus at my level of experience; my future at the company was bright. The mortgage-backed securities giant had taken a chance on a young kid with no experience in finance three years earlier, and I was quickly making my mark. At face value, there was no reason to reconsider my employment at the company.

But the job was just not for me. What was once my dream had become my greatest source of unhappiness. My family and friends begged me to reconsider my decision to leave the lucrative position with such a respected company. "You want to be a day trader?" my dad angrily puzzled. But my mind was already made up. It was the most uncertain moment of my life, but I have never felt as free as I did that day. That phone call from my best friend helped make my decision a little easier. Even as a youth, I knew in my heart that I was an entrepreneur. Trading, more than any other business, is purely entrepreneurial. As a trader, you truly reap what you sow.

T3 TIP ·

Trading is the most entrepreneurial job you can have. To have success, you must treat it like a small business.

Growing up, I did not know I would become a trader, or even what stocks were, but my entrepreneurial instincts first appeared early on. In third grade, my school held a bake sale where the students sold cupcakes and cookies to raise money. Everyone else was content to sit quietly at their booth and sell their baked goods. Not me. I wanted an edge; I wanted to win. So I devised a plan. In addition to providing samples at my booth, I sent my loyal foot soldiers out to other booths with samples to entice patrons to buy from me. At the end of the day, I closed up shop without a crumb of inventory remaining as my classmates wondered what to do with all their leftover treats. I was already beating the street. My teacher marveled at what I would realize many years later while sitting behind a desk at Greenwich:

"When you grow up, you should be an entrepreneur."

BEING PROACTIVE

All my life I have pushed the envelope. While other people may settle for what is comfortable, I put myself out there. The audacity that revealed itself as a precocious nine-year-old salesman foreshadowed what would make me a successful trader. Throughout my life, my mother has emphasized to me that it is okay to make mistakes. "You should make mistakes. The more you make, the more you learn," she would tell me. I have carried that lesson with me. My ability to overcome missteps and embrace change is the reason I am where I am today, and I wouldn't have it any other way. As of the writing of this book, I am only 35 years old, but feel like I have made 60 years worth of mistakes. Whenever I feel stale, I try something new. The reason I am still in trading is because there is no limit to how far you can push yourself as a trader. I continue to try new things and challenge myself to be better every day.

T3 TIP ···
Nothing will ever be given to you. Go out and take what you want.
··

There are two types of people in the world: talkers and doers. In no setting is it easier to separate the two than on a trading floor. Numbers do not lie. Trading is a difficult business, but a complete meritocracy. Winners and losers are judged solely on profits and losses. If you are self-motivated and a good personality fit for trading, you have the chance to achieve great success.

The other great lesson I learned as a youth that has served me well in my trading career is the importance of being proactive, being a "doer." If you are reactionary, trades will pass you by and you will be left wondering why you are not in the stock that just ran up ten percent, or even worse, in it late as it comes crashing back down. My parents made a point of never helping me land a job, thus forcing me to be proactive in my career. They believed that some of the most important lessons were learned from the search itself, and I have to agree.

SEEKING SUCCESS

In trading and in life, it is important to have people to emulate and aspire to their success. When I started my trading career, the business was young and formal training was an after-thought. If you were smart, you latched onto the best trader at your firm and followed his every word. Throughout my life, I have been fortunate enough to have mentors who taught me valuable lessons at each step in my journey.

T3 TIP ....
The best way to learn trading is still to seek out the top professionals to learn from.

My first mentor was my tennis coach Gary Sciarella, who started training me when I was seven years old. When we trained, he always stressed the value of a strong work ethic, both as a tennis player and a person. If I was struggling with my forehand, I would stay late and hit 100 forehands. If my serve was not powerful enough, I would carefully reexamine my grip.

Trading is no different. While personality is a factor in success, a solid work ethic is vital to becoming profitable. As a young trader, I suffered losses, but instead of putting my head down, I was the first one in the office and the last one to leave every day. There are strong parallels between trading and sports, and former athletes often make great traders. I still like to play amateur hockey in organized leagues in my spare time and my style of play greatly resembles my approach as a trader. I am aggressive—I often lead the league in penalty minutes—and skilled; I generally lead the league in points scored, too. While it is in my nature to be hard-hitting and uncompromising, I have worked hard to hone my technique. A brash attitude and a commitment to improvement are qualities necessary, but not sufficient, to become a great trader.

Growing up, my family was always comfortable when it came to money, but nothing was ever given to me. While many of my friends received large allowances from their parents, mine made me work to keep up. Not wanting to work at a typical minimum wage job, I leveraged my years of tennis training into a job as a tennis instructor. As my friends were soaking up the sun at the beach, my shirt was soaking up sweat while I lobbed balls over the net to older ladies at a local country club. I did not resent my situation. The long days in the summer heat did not break my spirit; on the contrary, they kindled a fire in me to do something more. Working with wealthy country club types presented a great opportunity to network with influential people. I was always thinking outside the box, looking for ways to get ahead. While most people would have gone through the motions, my brain was always working. That outside-the-box thinking would eventually pay off.

FIRST TASTE OF TRADING

I first heard about trading stocks out on those tennis courts. Everyone was buzzing about the stock market, including my students. I wanted to get a piece of this action. To be perfectly honest, I did not know the first thing about the stock market at that time. I wanted to invest some of my savings into the market, but did not really know where to start. I eventually followed the advice of famous investor Peter Lynch. Lynch, author of several books on investing, popularized the idea of "invest in what you know." Basically, pick stocks based on conversations at a cocktail party or when you are out to dinner. If a company has a product people like, or people around you have "local knowledge" of a promising company, you the individual are well-positioned to take advantage.

I applied the theory loosely, simply picking five technology stocks I had either read about or heard about from one of my tennis students. Lucky for me, my first foray into the markets came at a time when it was nearly impossible to lose money. In fact, it was harder to lose money than to make it. Throwing darts at a board of stocks and buying the ones they hit would have made money. The infamous E*Trade Super

Bowl commercial depicted monkeys making money trading, and it was not a far off idea. The dot-com boom was making people fortunes, and a flood of opportunists saturated the trading world. As a naïve teen, I made ten times my initial investment, so you can imagine what kinds of returns the professionals were seeing. That initial taste of success made me hungry for more. Not only did I make money, it was exciting! At that point, I decided that I wanted to be involved in the financial markets.

"Invest in what you know."

-Peter Lynch

THE JOURNEY BEGINS

I earned a Bachelor of Arts degree in economics from the University of Michigan, where I learned the basics of business. I learned how to write a business plan and how the global economy worked. But I needed to get out there to really learn. As Mark Twain once said, "Never let school get in the way of your education." Although I would soon return to school to get my MBA, it was the professional journey I was most looking forward to. Armed with my entrepreneurial spirit and proactive approach, it was time to start throwing things against the wall and see what stuck.

My initial goal was to become an investment banker. Investment banking is a magnet for the top minds in finance, so naturally it was my first inclination to get involved in this highly competitive industry. If you are successful, it can be a stepping stone to even larger arenas. Many of the most revered junior analysts go on to huge salaries as hedge fund managers, their abilities handsomely rewarded early on in their career. The most ambitious characters gun for these I-banking internship positions. I did not know exactly what I wanted to do, but I had great ambition.

Unfortunately, I never got that prestigious internship. Although I landed a couple of interviews, an offer was never in the cards. I moved back home after school to again teach tennis lessons at my country club for another summer. I was sometimes anxious that I was not putting myself in the best position to succeed, but I would later discover a disdain for corporate culture that would have made me ill-suited to a banking career, anyway.

After graduating, many friends turned internships into lucrative full-time offers and scattered across the country to fill the same jobs I had initially sought. In the meantime, I continued to compile a very impressive collection of rejection letters. The most promising opportunity came from Solomon Brothers, who flew me to New York for a second round interview.

I had done well in school, but did not have the best grades or test scores. Most firms passed me over because of these average numbers. Solomon's recruiters, as others before, recognized my enthusiasm and intellect. This time I could taste it. As the conversation began, the interviewer asked me plainly, "What are your goals in this business and within our company?" These companies value ambition, I thought, something I had in abundant supply. Solomon wanted someone driven to succeed and advance. So my response was, "I want to work hard, move up, and make a lot of money." I will never forget the interviewer's face at that moment as it hardened in disbelief. Getting rich is not something to highlight as a central goal. My ambition was very misplaced, apparently. We continued with the interview, but it was a foregone conclusion that I had talked myself out of the job. Friends were flying high, and I had not even made it to the airport.

A WINDOW OPENS

As it turned out, my education on the tennis courts was not finished. Although my stock picks had worked out very well before, this time around I was in a position to more fully take advantage of opportunities. I soon realized the value of networking. I learned more about finance, the stock market, and life than I ever could have in a corporate job. My situation was not as hopeless as it first seemed. School was behind me; I had struck out in my quest for a job and was back lobbing balls over the net monotonously. But I was always engaging people, especially if they had any connection to a potential job. I knew my big break would show its face eventually, and it came sooner than expected.

Among my tennis students were the wife and kids of Gary Holloway, the CEO of Greenwich Capital Markets, one of the largest players in the mortgage-backed securities world. His wife recognized my work ethic and our conversations revealed my intellect, so I followed up on several conversations with her and gained the opportunity to interview with the company. After one interview with human resources, the mutual fit was clear. I was hired into the risk management group for the hedge fund sector. I truly loved that job.

My boss, Bill Gallagher, took a special interest in me from the start. From him I learned my first lessons about managing people effectively. He taught me what it meant to treat people fairly and how to engender loyalty and productivity. We developed a close bond and he was quick to offer advice, even to his detriment. When I expressed a desire to grow within the company, he realized that I had outgrown my position and needed to move on. Although loathe to see me go, Bill said that if I wanted to move up, I needed to move on to the trading floor. So that is what I did.

T3 TIP ···

Change is an inevitable part of life and trading; you must be willing and able to adapt.

MOVING UP

As the youngest trader in the firm at the time, many of the senior traders took exception to my early success. I did not let the resentment faze me, instead working harder to prove my worth. When my bonus that year eclipsed that of many older traders, things really got stuffy in the room. "Wonder Boy," they called me. Some used the nickname out of respect, but most out of spite. It got old very fast. The jabs soon crossed the line into disrespect. "Get me a cup of coffee," a senior manager barked one day, "and bring me back some ice cream too." After my promotion to vice president, it got to a tipping point. I was earning a good salary while possessing great power and autonomy, but knew I could not stay at the company. The pitfalls of corporate bureaucracy were now staring me in the face. I no longer had the desire to do the job, and never would again.

MOVING ON

And then the phone rang. Disillusioned after three years at GCM despite moving up quickly, my desire to be an entrepreneur was even stronger. Trading provided a great outlet for my resourcefulness. My friend trained me in the same methods that had made him wealthy. I found the markets fascinating and exciting, and worked hard to learn the craft. It was definitely the most exciting time of my life. As any trader would tell you, it is a very unique and powerful feeling sitting in front of that computer screen with millions in buying power at your fingertips. It is almost like you can make money appear out of thin air. The feeling is almost surreal at first.

Soon I too would be making $300,000 in a day, I thought. I was eager, bursting with optimism. Putting $50,000 of the money earned in my three years at Greenwich into a trading account, I got to work. Every last penny was gone in two months. I had learned my lessons and would correct my mistakes. I had been overly eager, too aggressive and naïve to think I could just start making money instantly. Success would come next time, surely. I put $25,000 more in the account. It was gone in two weeks.

T3 TIP ···
Delusions of grandeur are a road to failure in trading.

At that point in my life, I was lower than low. I had given up a great job with the sky as the limit in terms of my growth potential. Even though I loathed the suffocating corporate environment, the stability of a job where you have a guaranteed income is—let's just say—a little more reassuring

> *The ways you respond to adversity determine what your life will become.*

than trading. I had been a rising star at GCM. And I had given it up for what, the chance to throw my money away? Trading was a mirage. Only a small number of people actually make money trading in the long run. Optimism turned to bottomless regret. My father had been right; daytrading was a crapshoot, it was gambling.

Anyone who has ever attempted trading knows the feeling. There is nothing like it. I knew when I got into the business that it was not for the faint of heart. I thought I was ready for the inevitable struggles, but you can never understand the feeling of losing so much money until it actually happens. All traders will experience adversity, and it is how you respond to that adversity that determines what your life will become. Although my anger and initial disappointment was overwhelming, I was not ready to give up. I liked coming to work too much to fail at this. Each morning waking up hungry to improve my trading, I put in the work to make it happen. Little by little, I was committed to building myself back up.

The satisfaction of success, of finally getting it, is what makes trading so special. The perilous journey to earning consistent profits in the business makes the destination that much more gratifying. Most begin their trading careers on a simulator, paper trading with no real capital. Eager rookies find paper trading easy, getting in and out of positions without the inevitable limitations of the real market. When they go "live," newfound trading egos are quickly put in check.

Dreams of sports cars and vacation homes quickly vanish as these traders take early losses, some not making it past the first few months. If your personality is a good fit for trading, and you are willing to put in the work to get better, the breakthrough is as inevitable as the early struggles. You just start to get it. The volatile movement in the market begins to make sense, the numbers on the computer screen begin to slow down, and the charts start to look like roadmaps. The trader morphs into a confident, calculated animal.

My transformation came as the walls were closing in faster than ever. The grief over my questionable decision to leave Greenwich was at an all-time high, but profits began to erase my doubts. In the months after losing that $75,000, I made it all back. Seeing green in the Profit and Loss box has that unique ability to clarify uncertainty. Full of the confidence and savvy that had driven me to success at GCM, I began to see healthy profits each month. The next $100,000 came early into my second year.

HIGH STRESS AND SUCCESS

The trading floor is littered with unique characters. Elite traders are some of the shrewdest thinkers and biggest hot-heads out there. Many are thrill-seeking types, some replicating the adrenaline of former athletic glory days through the biggest emotional roller coaster out there—the stock market. There is no other business where you can see tens of thousands of dollars appear and then disappear so quickly. The swings are often too much for some psyches. Temper tantrums are more common than in day care, although the business has grown more professional over the course of my career.

In the early days, I saw some legendary meltdowns. Chairs would fly around the room accompanied by obscenity-laced tirades. Fist fights were rare, but people often took exception to others' childish behavior. Heated exchanges were daily occurrences. Distracted one second because of a flying chair, you can miss a move in an open position, costing you thousands of dollars. If there was a time to get in someone's face, it was when they began to affect your livelihood. The only time I really took exception to flare-ups is when they cost me money.

It got to the point of expecting outbursts each day. Now, only the most colorful eruptions are still etched in my mind. One of those memories recalls the day that a particularly bright trader decided it was his keyboard's fault that he continued to lose money. He picked it up and smashed it into the table over and over, the keys flying around the room like shrapnel. After his tirade was over, panic set in. "I need a keyboard! I can't get out of my positions," he screamed. The trader's distress fell on deaf ears as his losses grew. As one of the victims of these airborne keys, I wanted to get up and punch the idiot in the face, but my cooler head prevailed. Besides, I was already up big on the day. The guy had felt enough pain, losing nearly $20,000 dollars because he felt the need to destroy his keyboard. I felt not an ounce of pity for guys like him.

My success did not come without some unfortunate days of my own. Always looking for better trading platforms—software essential for trading—I agreed to try out a company's new system. There was no harm, I thought, in trading just a small amount on the new platform. As I gave the command to buy 100 shares of Qualcomm (QCOM), the software maxed out my account, buying five million dollars worth of stock. Panicked, I tried to sell, but the computer sold the shares in addition to short selling five million more dollars of the stock. Back and forth it went; I could not get my position flat but rather was forced try to chop up the action as the technicians tried to fix the problem. At one point, I was down as much as $80,000 in the trade, but was able to work it back to a $20,000 loss. Still, I was distraught. "Don't worry about it," the owner of the software company said. "Not a big deal." The guy still hoped we would use his software, and he absorbed the $20,000 loss in stride. Losing $20,000 in five minutes is not a big deal? I wanted to be able shrug off losing that kind of money. It was not about the money, though. It was about what it meant to be able to roll with losses. The day I could do that was the day I would arrive as a successful trader. And that day did come. I became one of the top traders at my firm, and the time came for me to explore additional revenue streams.

ON YOUR OWN

When you are a highly successful and respected trader, new opportunities present themselves to you. Some traders are content to trade under another company, but I never saw myself as just a trader. By the time I had reached that level, I had earned my Masters of Business Administration degree in entrepreneurship and marketing from New York University's Stern School of Business, and possessed the skills and knowledge necessary to start my own firm. Armed with significant capital from my early trading exploits, that is exactly what I did.

In the trading business, it is often difficult to find people you can truly trust. I fully understood the pitfalls of managing your own company, and I set out on my way. The results, to be honest, were mixed. I entered into a few different partnerships but still did not find the right fit. As soon as I felt a venture had become stale, I worked to improve it or moved on. I tried many different things hoping to find the best option going forward. Focused and driven on a day-to-day basis, I always had one eye on the future.

Sometimes, my thirst for change and growth diverted me from what I was good at and enjoyed. After several proprietary trading partnerships, I decided to try my hand at managing my own hedge fund. Amassing $15 million dollars from investors (mainly close friends and family), I took a stab at managing other people's money. Managing this larger size was difficult and felt clumsy for me. The demands of the investors made me feel like I was back in a corporation with bosses telling me what to do. Managing the capital of others was not my strength. Although achieving mild success, I soon shut down the fund, returning the money to my investors.

It was back to square one, but I was excited as ever. As a manual proprietary trader, you are limited in terms of how many positions you can trade and how much capital you can manage. You are only one person, so it is impossible to stretch your earning potential beyond a certain point. I needed something where I could manage more positions and larger amounts of capital. Starting a traditional hedge fund was my attempt at growing the scope of my trading activities. I found the practice cumbersome and the demands of investors limiting. I needed something more nimble.

HIGH-FREQUENCY TRADING

High-frequency trading had been around for only a short amount of time when I discovered it, but new technologies and an evolving market made it the wave of the future. It was clear to me what my next step would be, and I could see that it would not be easy. In automated or "black box" trading, a computer automatically trades after being given decision-making criteria based on a specific trading strategy. Needless to say, computers possess certain advantages over human beings. The most difficult aspect of trading is the mental approach, and a computer obviously eliminates all biases. The 90/10 rule in trading estimates trading as 90 percent mental. The other important human limitation in trading is speed. Not only can a computer execute an individual trade much faster than a human can after being presented with specific conditions, it can execute trades in many different stocks. Teaming up with the brightest programmers I could find, I used the name that defined my corporate frustrations as inspiration for my new company. WB (Wonder Boy) Capital was born.

Black boxes are programmed with all different types of strategies, from longer-term swing to micro-scalping, to high frequency. The computer buys or sells smaller lots of a diverse collection of stocks that fit the criteria of the trading system, hedging against risk while possibly providing significant returns. Automated trading is now a large part of T3's business operation. The growth of high-frequency trading will likely continue, leading to a more liquid and efficient marketplace for everyone. Rather than squeeze out manual traders, a more electronic market will reward the most disciplined and educated traders and investors.

T3 TIP ···
High-frequency trading is the future of the markets, but manual traders will always have their place.

MOVING FORWARD

The common theme in my life has been never standing still, but always moving forward. From networking on the tennis court to entering the high-frequency trading realm, I have always worked to advance myself each and every day. T3 Live is a highly successful business enterprise, but we are not resting on our laurels. We will continue to grow each aspect of our business as well as explore new opportunities. T3 Live in particular is on the cutting edge of trading and trading education. The evolution of the Internet and social networking has presented new opportunities for individual traders to interact and share information. In this new era, the most successful individuals will be the ones who take advantage of the extensive resources and technology now at their disposal.

4

Marc Sperling
The Natural

EIGHT MONTHS INTO MY CAREER AT OLDE DISCOUNT Brokers, my boss told me he would be holding a sales competition between me and his other assistant broker. The two of us had always been very competitive, battling for praise and the chance to move up in the company. The contest winner would be the front-runner for a full-fledged broker position and we both knew it. But just as the competition got under way, I got sick.

At age 15, doctors had diagnosed me with Crohn's Disease, an auto-immune gastrointestinal disease characterized by extreme bouts of abdominal pain, vomiting, and weight loss. The disease has no cure or surgical remedy—treatment is generally limited to controlling symptoms and preventing relapse. It was often incapacitating in college; most any night out was followed by a day of unbearable pain. It was hard to for my friends to see me in such pain, but no disease would prevent me from living my life.

The worst flare-up came as I was to begin that all-important sales contest at Olde. The pain was agonizing, but I didn't want to take time off. The competitive spirit that has always raged inside of me wanted to push on. This was a golden opportunity for me to move up in the company. In the end, the episode became too acute for me to continue. After urging from my family, I went to the doctor. My condition worsened and doctors recommended surgery. Surgery removed a quarter of my colon and much of the small intestine. I remained in the hospital for 11 long days recovering from the procedure, thinking about the missed opportunity. Eight months into my career, my life hit a major roadblock.

The more you pity yourself, the more debilitating adversity becomes. I never felt sorry for myself; although my disease was painful, I did not blame anyone or sulk. This disease had hurt my career, the worst attack coming at the worst possible time. It would have been easy to let it consume me, not only the pain, but the fact that it would continue to hinder my career. I chose to take a different path. ABC—Adversity Builds Character—the adage claims. And I agree. I was finally able to get back to work at Olde and forge a successful career with the company, more motivated than ever to be the best. My struggles with Crohn's disease forced me to become a man. Instead of letting the setbacks get me down,

> *The more you pity yourself, the more debilitating adversity becomes.*

I used them as motivation. The hard work and discipline it took to overcome the pain hardened me into a mentally tough person.

FOUNDATIONS

My experiences growing up helped to cultivate the personality traits that make me a dynamic trader and person. My parents were always supportive of me. Neither of them had any background in business, so I was not pushed into it by any means. During high school I developed a fascination with the financial world and was eager to learn more. Working as a waiter, I read discarded financial sections of the local newspaper to begin my market education. Well before beginning my own trading career, I read stories about people making fortunes trading stocks. The more I learned, the more appealing it sounded. I did not know much—like why the market moved or how I could profit from it—but I was itching to learn more. I had no idea the path I took would lead to something that fits my personality and skill set like a glove. My journey to become a trader was as random as anyone else's. Consistent trading success has more to do with personality and temperament and less to do with intelligence and knowledge, so traders come from all walks of life.

I graduated from Ithaca College in upstate New York with a degree in marketing before returning home to Philadelphia. At the time, the symptoms from Crohn's were starting to appear more often, the pain becoming more debilitating. The first full-time job I pursued was for a Gentleman's Officer position with Club Med. Basically, the job entails traveling to tropical destinations with the company, working as part tour guide, part designated partier. It is a dream job in the truest sense of the words, and would be a chance to travel, relax, enjoy life, and hopefully limit my symptoms in a low-stress environment.

While waiting for a position to open up, I waited tables and served as a counselor for a company that took groups on camping trips. While earning some money, I was disappointed I still had not gotten the call from Club Med, so began to look for other jobs. Hoping to gain exposure to the stock market, I pursued several finance jobs. I eventually landed one, an entry-level stock broker position at home in Philadelphia. Olde Discount Brokers was one of the first discount brokerages. Discount brokers were a hot concept and the company was leading the revolution. The firm was full of young motivated people like me, so it was an exciting place to potentially start a career.

However, soon after I got the offer from Olde, a call came from Club Med—a G.O. position opened up. I was truly torn. The two paths could not have been more different, both holding their own appeal. I could take the job with Club Med and sail around in paradise, or start with Olde working long days in a corporate office. On the surface the decision was a no-brainer; I was young and had plenty of time to make money and work office jobs. However, I had a hunch that I would enjoy work as a broker. I wanted to learn about the market. In the end, I decided it was time for me to begin my career, so I turned down Club Med and went to work for Olde. In my first couple of years at the firm, I second-guessed myself often, but given where the path has led me, it is impossible to have any doubts now about the choice.

IOMEGA GUY

I had achieved my goal of getting into finance, and was hopeful of soon learning the secrets to making a fortune in the stock market. Clearly, I did not understand how brokerages worked. Many things about the job felt empty. First of all, I never realized how much selling was involved. I was never a born salesman, nor did I want to be. I hated asking people for money. Secondly, the senior brokers knew little more than I did about how to consistently make money in the stock market. Buy and hold investing seemed like somewhat of a crapshoot. The only real secret was there was no secret at all. The element of luck struck me as too central to the success of a broker, but fortunately for me it was on my side.

T3 TIP ··
The only secrets that exist in the brokerage world are that there are no secrets at all.

Missing out on the aforementioned sales competition my boss had arranged really set me back, but I was able to return to health and began to excel at work. After achieving mild success trading stocks for the company after my surgery, one day in 1995 really kick-started my career. I learned about a company called Iomega that had just introduced a portable storage device for personal computers. I did not perform any advanced research or analysis, it simply seemed like a good idea to me. I bought the stock hoping I had finally found a winner. I entered the stock at $10 and the price quickly spiked. I still liked the stock long, so I bought more and more on margin. The momentum never slowed; the stock ballooned day after day. I knew I was onto something big and I threw all the buying power I had behind the young company, including 10,000 of my own dollars. As the price continued to grow, I started to become known as "Iomega Guy."

My investment skyrocketed, but it was not all smooth sailing. When you get killed in the market, it feels like a punch in the stomach, and that is what it felt like when Iomega started its pullback. Iomega performed unreasonably well for so long, I thought it would never go down. I was inexperienced and probably a little greedy as a young broker, so I continued to add to my position. One day, as the market pulled in hard on some bad economic news, the stock lost 17 points. The pull-in translated to a $500,000 loss on my now enormous position. I was distraught. I eventually closed out the position for tremendous capital gains, but it was still an alarming feeling. The slight slip-up did not slow my rise to stardom within the company. As a 23-year-old broker who had been at the firm for only a year and a half, I had been transformed into somewhat of an icon. Everyone asked for tips. "What is Iomega Guy trading today?" The funny thing is I had done nothing different than before I was the "Iomega Guy." The fact that it was blind luck made the success unfulfilling.

The Iomega Guy sensation was not limited to my Philadelphia office. Stock brokers in the firm working at offices around the country inquired as to what I was trading each day. Only years after leaving the firm did I hear stories of how deep the obsession with Iomega Guy went. Other Olde offices around the country often took note of and my mirrored trades. Although I became more consistent with my picks, it still astonished me that brokers were so fixated on my trades simply because of my luck on one stock. The district manager made it a habit of riding my coattails. When friction developed with my manager as a result of my success, I knew that soon I would have to move on.

NEW YORK, NEW IDENTITY

I spent another couple of years at Olde after moving to their New York office. While I enjoyed being at home in Philadelphia, there was nothing like living in New York City as young man. Olde's New York office was downtown next to the stock exchange in what was dubbed the "Fish Bowl." The area got that name because every day you walk into work, you run into a sea of people. I became friendly with many of the brokers on Wall Street and struck up lasting relationships with others. The experience was great, but I once again wanted more out of my career.

Success as the Iomega Guy was due to luck. I had been fortunate to choose the most explosive of the strong tech stocks and was now mistaken for a genius. The circus had traveled far enough; my career as a broker had run its course. I had learned much about the markets in my time at the company but trying to please customers and coworkers had become too much of a strain. At the time, there were two choices: move on to another firm, or take a shot at trading my own capital. Why should I continue to be a broker? I wanted to dig deeper to find out if there was a more sure-fire way to consistently make money in the market. After hearing about a daytrading firm, Broadway Trading, from a colleague I had met in the Fish Bowl, I quit my job at Olde.

Broadway Trading was one of the first firms of its kind, providing the platform and space for individuals to trade but little in the way of training or financial backing. Surrounded by Wall Street veterans, I tried to soak up as much wisdom as possible. I was the new young gun, a confident kid who wanted it all. I thought I was ready. The brief time as a broker just after college inflated my ego as I achieved success picking stocks during the internet boom. Armed with supreme overconfidence and tidbits of advice picked up from senior traders at Broadway, I put six figures into a prop account to trade. It was a common tale of tragic failure waiting to happen. After hearing stories about fortunes being made in the stock market, a naïve young professional puts it all on the line and loses everything. I was basically thrown into the ring with no knowledge of how to fight. The market definitely put me back in my place.

T3 TIP ···
Before you try your hand at trading or managing your own
money, make certain you have the proper education.
···

Especially in trading, it is important to have thick skin and unyielding optimism. If setbacks lead to paralysis, if failures consume you, then being a good trader is impossible. Trading is full of failures, and I certainly had my share. With no formal training, I began my trading career. I lost almost $30,000 in six weeks. The pain of throwing away so much money consumes most people and pushes them out of the business back into the rat race. Much like there is for a stock, there is a pivot point where a young trader can sink or swim. The ones that eventually flourish combine an innate self-belief with the commitment to put in the work it takes to be successful. A good trader is supremely confident and despite early setbacks, my mindset was that it was a matter of when, not "if" I would become a successful trader.

If setbacks lead to paralysis, if failures consume you, then being a good trader is impossible.

FROM BROKER TO TRADER

The beginning of a stock trader's career can be a trying time. The losing days can test your strength of will. Many suffer losses that force them out of trading. My early days trading followed a similar path. Despite some early struggles, it took relatively little pain before turning it around, thanks to the craziness of the tech bubble. The dot-com boom of the late '90s made geniuses out of everyone. Trading became a lucrative and sexy way to get rich quick. If you bought and held a quality technology stock, you were almost guaranteed to see lofty returns. It was a challenge to lose money. I was fortunate to begin my trading career during such a lucrative time in the markets. As an independent and competitive guy, the business of trading suited me a lot better than working as a broker.

The transition to trading does not work for most brokers because the attitude and thought processes are entirely different. Early on in my trading career, I relied a lot on the Wall Street veterans that populated the trading floor. Although the philosophy underlying investing and trading are certainly different, a broker's intimate knowledge of the market and institutions are a great advantage. Still, knowing the difference is important. Relying on the shaky advice from former brokers is what got me into an early hole. Traditional value investing revolves around fundamental analysis. Fundamentals can be a tool in trading, but standing alone, they are far from a good indicator for future prices in the short or intermediate-term. Fundamental analysis is considered safer, and as a broker, it drives your decision making. After starting at Broadway Trading, I was forced to shift gears.

Active trading employs an entirely different type of decision making on a much shorter time frame. While fundamental analysis can be the study of what stocks should do, technical analysis is the study of what they actually do. Technical analysis involves the use of price levels and stock charts to determine imminent price action. The same patterns begin to appear in the charts and predict price movement. Each pattern carries with it a psychology that explains why it happens, but knowing how stocks react to each pattern is most important. Along with other complementary tools, price levels, patterns, and volume analysis better predict price action than any other type of analysis.

Stock charts are simply a visual representation of prices. In the early days of trading, they were not commonplace, so it was more difficult to analyze price action in stocks. Looking at streaming stock prices, traders determined levels of support, resistance, and patterns in stocks, and it took a quick mind to be able to analyze the data fast enough. I was able to draw lots of information from prices more quickly than others, and my trading was likewise more efficient. When stock charts became the norm, my trading went to another level. Now, with charts, I am able to trade dozens of stocks at one time, my well-trained eye requiring only a glance for me to identify a compelling pattern.

THE LIGHT BULB

Every trader experiences a defining moment that sets the stage for growth and long-term profitability. The light bulb suddenly goes on as a trader learns from mistakes and takes note of how successes were achieved. I remember my turning point vividly.

Fundamental analysis can provide insight as to what stocks should do, while technical analysis is the study of what they actually do.

Although I love hockey, I could not pay attention to the action that night at the Flyers game. Home in Philadelphia at the game with my brother, my mind was somewhere else. That day, I had made $16,500 trading. The eagerly-awaited breakthrough had finally come. The desire to get back to my trading desk tortured me. I am sure I annoyed my brother talking about it. Maybe my enthusiasm that night is the reason he came to work with me for a time before pursuing a career in the field of psychology. I could not sleep when we got home; the idea of making that much money in one day blew my mind. Restless, at 5:00 a.m., I jumped off my brother's couch and woke him up to say I was cutting my trip short. "I have to get back," I said, "to see if I can do it again."

The next day, I made $64,000. Lying awake the night before at my brother's apartment, I was full of questions. Did I really just make that much money? Had I discovered the secret to conquering the markets? Could I do it again? The next day brought the realization: There was no limit to the money I could make in the stock market.

SUCCESS AND SETBACKS

Even after the light went on, there was still adversity. No matter how long you have been the business, you will experience devastating setbacks. A most painful loss transpired a couple years into my trading career. At this point I was making good money, generally a few thousand dollars a day, but five figure days were not uncommon. My biggest loss to that point was around $30,000. I was beginning to gain confidence, throwing around more and more share size. That particular day, I was flipping around five to ten thousand shares of Amazon (AMZN). Things were going fine, until suddenly the system locked up and I could no longer control my positions. The computer was filling orders on a delayed basis, and I could not cancel them. Back and forth it went. Each time I was losing money on the spread and price movement of the stock. It is hard to imagine the panic that overcomes you when your trading system goes haywire unless you have been in that situation. You are in millions of dollars of stock and can only watch helplessly as your account gets decimated. Next thing I know, *** came up in my Profit and Loss box. Although I had never seen it before, I knew immediately what it meant. Star, star, star. It meant I had accumulated six-figure losses for the day. I eventually was able to close out all my positions, but the damage was done. At the end of the day, I had lost six figures. Needless to say, I was distraught.

There was no limit to the money I could make in the stock market.

The loss was largely the result of a computer error, but it did not matter. I had just lost more money than I had ever made in a two month span. It was impossible not to be angry; I went home that day fuming. While losses in the first weeks of my trading career had been hard to swallow, this disaster was going to be hard to come back from. But while going home on tilt, I knew I needed to cool myself down. I went out with some friends, had a few drinks and cleared my head. I made up my mind to fight. I had overcome a lot to get to this point and I could not let one bad day ruin me. If the excruciating pain of Crohn's Disease did not dictate my life, why would I let one bad day determine the course of my career?

The three days following the carnage are my proudest in trading. I came into the office with a renewed focus. I made a concerted effort to maintain discipline while still being aggressive. I had never made six figures in a day to that point. Based on past performance, it would take me two great months, at least, to erase the losses from that day. The task was tall, but I was confident that by plugging away each day, I would eventually get there. I went back to the office, took a deep breath, and set off on a mission.

In just three days, I had made back all of that money, and then some. I was amazed at what I had done. Everyone in the office was amazed. I still take great pride being able to pull off that comeback. I did not bellyache like most in that situation might have. I was angry, but I did not make excuses. The confidence drawn from that run paved the way for me to become the trader I am today.

In my first year as a professional stock trader, I made around a quarter of a million dollars. My monster days were sometimes followed by days of big losses caused mostly by reckless hunger. Still, nothing was going to stop me from being the best. In 1998, my second year as a trader, I made one million dollars. The next year, I made two million dollars, and there was no looking back. Despite forging a successful trading career, it is not purely the money that I am most proud of. I take pride in overcoming adversity. I value the relationships I have built along the way. Trading is a difficult business, and I have been able to overcome obstacles and adapt to changing environments that doomed others to failure. I have seen just about every kind of market and done extremely well in each. Although my trading success is the result of hard work, it has always come somewhat naturally.

Broadway Trading was full of guys like me, talented brokers who became disillusioned and craved something better, a place where they could realize their full potential. The success I enjoyed in the first couple of years earned me a reputation within the company. I have always been somewhat risk averse, and my ability to maximize gains while minimizing danger defined my success. Although there were days of significant loss, they were few and far between. On two hands I can count the days I lost money the first two years. I built a solid foundation to continue my growth as a trader. As I continued to get better, my competitiveness with those around me grew. I wanted to be better than the next guy; I wanted to be the best.

I had been forced to enter the business with little training, trading my own capital, so I wanted to provide traders with guidance and support. I started my own trading firm, Sperling Enterprises, and set about molding new traders in my image. Management was never my forte, and the company was admittedly poorly managed at times. While we consistently made money, the organizational side was haphazard. The firm was successful because of the quality of traders and the environment we were able to create. Everyone at the firm had a lot of fun everyday they came into work. The camaraderie of a young, successful trading floor is like a professional sports locker room. It was group of dynamic and energetic young people driven to be the best. The lifestyle we forged was exciting and the relationships we built have been lifelong. I remain close to most all of the traders who were with Sperling Enterprises during those great years, and many of them were in my wedding. The bonds we built and the experiences we shared were reminiscent of a fraternity. We had all been through the fire and made it out on the other side. We enjoyed the good times together, and suffered through the tough times like brothers.

TRANSITIONS

As my career progressed, I began investing in other things I enjoyed. Since my days as a waiter, I had always held an interest the restaurant business. I invested in many restaurants with varying degrees of success. To this day, I still own a stake in the wildly successfully sushi restaurant, Sushi Samba. Along with friends in the trading business, I also invested in concert tours, a venture that led to some memorable adventures. I met many top record company producers, and many chart-topping artists as I traveled around the country "monitoring" my investment. After investing in one of his tours, I found myself having a conversation with P. Diddy before he went on stage.

The first decade of my trading career was truly unforgettable. After a particularly rich stretch of trading, I went on the trip of a lifetime with four of my closest trading buddies. We had all been enjoying tremendous success and figured it would not hurt to take time off during the summer months when trading volume and volatility decreases. In reality, the weeks we missed were great for trading, but at that point we did not really care.

We rented a yacht with full staff and traveled throughout the Mediterranean. We visited Barcelona and Greece. We swam freely around the boat in between voyages to many of the beautiful Greek Isles. It was one of many amazing trips we took. We took excursions to Miami and a trip to Cannes, France. That was life during the technology boom. The money people were making was surreal. Traders became numb to putting up hundred thousand dollar days.

Another trip I remember vividly came after the firm enjoyed one of its best weeks ever. Wanting to reward the traders for their performance, I arranged for buses to pick everyone up for an unforgettable night in Atlantic City. We partied, we gambled, and celebrated our good fortune like it was going out of style. What is success if you do not take time out to enjoy it? The traders appreciated the generosity and the trip served to further the strong sense of team and camaraderie we had developed.

As I have gotten older, my priorities have shifted. I am now married and have two children, and I derive my pleasure out of maintaining a strong marriage and providing a happy life for my kids. I take the time to be with family, to take the kids out to a movie, and to have dinner at home. Still, it is impossible not to remember those glory days.

The tech bubble had created something out of nothing. Money poured into unprofitable companies that promised to be the next big thing. In reality, all of the investment was creating a bubble that was poised to inevitably burst. As the market came down, many were pushed out of the business because they could not adapt to a different market environment. I had never really shorted stock much to that point, and although my strategy of buying dips worked sometimes, I too lost large amounts. The crash worked to trim the fat in the business and cut out those who were in the business for an easy buck. The traders remaining were the truly great traders, and it made for a much more efficient operation. At the time, trading was the sexy thing to do, and after the crash, that title shifted to real estate. Another bubble was created by the greedy masses who wanted to get rich quick.

In the world of trading, there are certainly gray areas. There are many different types of traders who hold positions over longer or shorter time periods. Scalpers try to capture momentum for small price movements and consistent gains. Swing traders take out larger positions and look for complete moves with follow-through based on technical chart patterns. I fall somewhere in between. Each trading strategy has its advantages and drawbacks; it is most important to find what works for you. Furthermore, it is important to recognize if trading itself is simply not for you.

Trading is like a puzzle. There are many different numbers and indicators you must use in order to see the whole picture, and you must be able to put all of the pieces together before you have a finished product. The makeup of a good trader is no different. You must have the personality type that allows you to never get too high or too low. Most people do not have the ability to separate emotions from rational thought and deal with misfortune.

Throughout my life, I have faced adversity and become a better, more dynamic person for it. Likewise, without hardship, I would never have become the trader I am today. My struggles with Crohn's disease made me a stronger and more resilient person. My setbacks in trading made me more motivated and driven. In life and in trading, you are sure to reach several points where you can either give up or fight. How you react in those moments makes all the difference.

5

Scott Redler
The Workhorse

AFTER SWIMMING 2.4 MILES AND BIKING MORE THAN 112 miles in the Lake Placid 2007 Ironman—one of the most grueling tests in all of sport—I was almost halfway through the final leg of the race, a full 26-mile marathon. It was one of the hottest days in Lake Placid history, and despite the oppressive heat, I felt great. Regularly passing other runners and cruising towards the head of the pack, a quick glance at my watch showed me that I was well on the way to beating my personal goal.

Eleven hours earlier, I had started the competition with hundreds of other competitors. Now less than half of them remained. Some could not finish the 2.4 mile swim, while others tired during the 112 mile bike ride. Many others could not summon the strength to even start the final run of 26 miles on wobbly legs already tortured beyond comprehension. As other competitors dropped out of the event, I kept running at a comfortable pace.

Suddenly, a sharp pain shot up my forearm. It quickly spread to the shoulder blade and sliced down my left leg. My left quadriceps seized up and tightened. After so many hours of training, waking up early every morning to stretch, jog, bicycle, and swim, my body had suddenly turned against me. The left side of my body went numb as my foot cramped and my trembling body crashed to the pavement with a thud.

Lying there on the road in the fetal position, my entire left side wracked with pain, I was unable to move. Racers I had passed by what seemed like ages ago were now galloping past as my body screamed in agony. "This can't be happening to me," I thought. I had trained too hard and sacrificed too much for it to end like this. Just moments earlier, I was dreaming about the finish line and seeing my family as I conquered what few have ever attempted. Now, I could not even think of standing, let alone running the final fifteen miles of the race. My dream lay shattered inside a body that had betrayed me.

Still lying helplessly on the ground writhing in pain, Steven's words echoed in my head. "I'll see you when you finish a real triathlon." My best friend Steven Perez never did see me finish a triathlon, and if he was still alive, he would have seen me trembling on the ground, failing to finish the race.

Thinking of Steven, hearing his words in my head, and picturing his face waiting at the finish line gave me the strength to begin to take back control of failing arms and legs. Another runner passed by, tossed a packet by my head, and said, "You need salt, buddy." Every racer carries salt packs. As your body burns its internal fuel, it loses water and salt. The lack of water leads to dehydration. A lack of salt leads to muscle seizures, which was exactly what I was experiencing.

Although the salt pack the other runner had tossed lay just inches from my head on the pavement, it might as well have been a million miles away. I could not reach it. I could not push my shaking hand out far enough to grab it. I closed my eyes and let another spasm of pain wash over me. That is when I thought about all I had been through, all I had trained for, all I had hoped for, and realized it was disappearing in one agonizing moment. I could not let it happen.

THE STARTING LINE

I began to think how it all began. I always enjoyed exercising and living a healthy lifestyle, but had gotten bored with my workout routine. To challenge myself, I decided to train for a sprint triathlon, which is about half as long as a normal one. The Oyster Bay Triathlon—a sprint class race—featured a half-mile swim, 11-mile bike ride and five-kilometer run. I invited all my friends and family members to watch me cross the finish line on the day of the race. However, I did not see my best friend, Steven Perez, who had been my roommate and best friend since our college days at SUNY Albany.

Disappointed, I called Steven and asked why he was not there. "Did you think I was going to give up my Saturday night to get up early and watch you do that?" Steven said to me. "I'll wake up early when you do a real triathlon." Laughing, I told him I would see him at my next race.

I had always thought about entering a "real" triathlon, but did not feel I had the right equipment or training. So for my 30th birthday, my girlfriend and future wife, Celena, threw a party where all my friends, at Steven's suggestion, chipped in and bought me a real racing bike. When Steven gave me the bike, he said, "Now you can think big and I'll be there when you finish a real triathlon." With a new bicycle, I started training in the spring of 2003 for my first triathlon. From the beginning, I knew I could do it and pictured myself in my first triathlon, watching Steven laugh as I crossed the finish line. But the dream never happened.

In May, Steven complained that he was feeling sick. Not thinking it was anything serious, he stayed home and waited to get better. When he failed to improve, he finally decided to see a doctor to for tests. The results were devastating.

The doctor told Steven he had a rare disease called Chronic Myelogenous Leukemia, or CML, and kept him in the hospital several weeks for more tests. I made it a point to visit him in the hospital as often as possible, and whenever I would show up, his relatives and several of his many friends were hanging out, trying to cheer him up. We would bring movies for him to watch and books for him to read. We even set up a putting green so he could practice in the hospital room. We knew he was facing a long and hard battle, but the doctors were treating it the best they could and we wanted to keep Steven's spirits up.

On August 4, just six weeks after Steven first learned of the disease, he suddenly passed away. The feeling hit me like a ton of bricks. The world lost one of the most amazing people I had ever known. A person who made an impression on everyone he met with his energy and liveliness, Steven was gone and I struggled to come to grips with the loss. I was not mature enough to handle losing someone so close to me. I was devastated. How could this happen to someone who was not even 30 years old?

I was depressed for a long time after Steven died. Every day I searched for answers. I searched for ways to move on with my life. Most of all, I looked for ways to honor his memory. I still remembered his words challenging me to enter a real triathlon. Exercise provided an outlet, a way to cope with the grief. I decided to enter a real triathlon and raise money for charity in honor of my best friend.

Setting a goal of $20,000, I picked out two charities to receive the money. The first was the New York City Chapter of the Leukemia & Lymphoma Society. The second was a foundation set up in his memory, the Steven M. Perez Foundation (www. smpfoundation.org). The foundation, among other things, provides scholarships to kids in the Long Island community where Steven and I grew up and sends those battling leukemia to camps to make their lives a little brighter. Initially, I thought triathlons would simply be a good escape for me and a way for me to remember my friend. I felt good about raising money to support the fight against cancer. I hoped the money I raised would give a kid with leukemia the fighting chance to survive that Steven never had. In the end, the effect it all had on my life was much greater than all those things. My life and career would change forever.

Values

Growing up, my family lived comfortably, but we were not wealthy. My parents moved to our neighborhood because it was in a good school district. They always valued education above all else. I developed a strong work ethic by working jobs throughout high school.

My parents were great role models. My dad worked long hours as a hairdresser, but no matter how long he worked, he always got everything done at home. He was up at 5:30 a.m. to walk the dog and do yard work before heading to a full day at his job. Once home, he cooked dinner and headed out to give haircuts around the neighborhood for additional income. He was happy to do whatever it took to make his family happy and comfortable.

My mom was always a source of encouragement for me. She wanted me to remember where I came from but also pushed me to achieve. While she instilled in me the importance of being humble and remembering my roots, she emphasized the need to strive for something greater.

Personality

People have always told me that I am a very sociable person. In high school, I had a lot of friends and began living a fast-paced lifestyle. I went on to attend the State University of New York in Albany, majoring in marketing and finance. I was a very active member of the SUNY-Albany community. After joining a fraternity, I was elected social chair and eventually President of my chapter. While pursuing a Bachelor of Arts degree, I earned spare money promoting nearby bars. As a promoter, I would bring customers to the bar and receive a percentage of the cover charge for each person I brought.

Besides promoting special events, I also worked nights and weekends as an emcee, entertaining guests at weddings and bar mitzvahs with the help of my roommate and best friend Steven Perez. Steven had a very gregarious personality like me, and from the day we met, we felt like brothers. We were joined at the hip, promoting events and networking with people every chance we could get. In college, I promoted a massive New Year's Eve party every year. By contacting the president of each fraternity and sorority in my school and getting them to sell tickets to the party, I was able to attract huge groups of people. The more tickets they sold, the more money each fraternity or sorority would collect for themselves, which in turn increased my bottom line. We all came out ahead.

The first New Year's Eve party I coordinated hosted over 1,500 people, which provided me with enough money to pay for the rest of my school expenses. I did this every year, and by my fourth year of college, my New Year's Eve parties had grown to over 2,700 people and was moved the Paramount Studios in Madison Square Garden to accommodate the swelling crowds. My New Year's Eve parties were even cited in a marketing textbook as an example of marketing through networking.

During summers, I continued to promote bars and nightclubs and to earn extra money, even working as a bartender in the same venues I promoted. After school each term, I chose not to move back in with my parents for the summer months, so Steven and I came up with a way for us to have a good time and make some money on the side. Each summer, we leased a big house in the Hamptons. Each house came with a swimming pool, hot tub, tennis court, basketball court, and outdoor barbecue grill. For three months, the lease totaled $45,000, obviously more than a college kid could afford.

We rented out rooms in the house for $1,500 a person, and got more than thirty people into those houses. All of our friends had a great place to live and a chance to have a good time all summer long. Best of all, the rent money more than paid for the cost of the house, giving Steven and I an extra $5,000 apiece. In addition, we invited all the people renting rooms in the Hamptons house to come to the bars and nightclubs I was promoting. Each of my business enterprises benefited the other. When the summer ended, it was back to school to start the whole routine over again.

All traders possess a strong sense of autonomy and motivation to make money on their own terms.

I feel my social life in college illustrates my approach to life as a whole. Being friendly comes naturally to me, and as I got older, I realized the true value of relationships. Trading works in much the same way. All traders possess a strong sense of autonomy and motivation to make money on their own terms. You have to be resourceful to have success, and my social exploits reinforced that quality in me.

NEXT STEPS

After graduating from college, like a lot of young kids, I wanted to enter the finance world. That is when an older friend of mine, who had become a trader at a small brokerage firm, suggested going to work at his small company. "You never like being just a number," he said, "and you always want to be in a situation where you can grow. You can come here, work hard, and eventually become a partner."

The idea of working in a smaller firm within a more entrepreneurial environment was appealing, so I took the job. I started out as a junior broker, and within a year and a half I had become a junior partner in the firm. I continued to promote parties all over New York City, Long Island, and the Hamptons during my off hours. Although I was excelling as a stock broker, it was not a perfect fit. I worked hard and most investments performed well for my clients, but I did not like having to sell others on my ideas. Being a broker was also frustrating to me because of the lag time between decision and execution. I might find a great stock opportunity, but by the time clients were contacted to hear the pitch, the good value entry price would be gone.

T3 TIP ···
Good traders are not always good brokers, because traders value more independent thinking.
··

Brokers hold onto the stock longer than they should, wiping out any of the small gains earned from winning stocks.

That mentality was frustrating to me. I wanted to do things my own way but I did not have that sort of authority. Working as a stock broker proved exasperating and disappointing. One thing was for sure: I was not a broker.

CHANGE OF PACE

A particular client of mine knew my promoting background and wondered aloud why I didn't focus on promoting full-time. With each passing day, I started to wonder the same thing."You've been promoting all of these New Year's Eve parties," he told me. "Why not take it up a level and promote something really big for a change?" My job as promoter was to pitch investors on concert tours that had the potential to return a profit of as much as 40 to 50 percent. I went to work for a company that specialized in promoting concerts and other large events. Within days, I was put in charge of promoting three Prince concerts. After raising $150,000 from investors, all three concerts sold out and my investors saw healthy returns. The opportunity to attend concerts by world-famous artists made the experience that much more rewarding. I even got a chance to meet Prince at one of the concert after-parties.

Following this initial success, I wound up promoting more and more concerts, including two in Atlantic City for James Brown, whom my friends and I also had a chance to meet. Then there was a Chubby Checkers concert and even one for Jeff Foxworthy in Albuquerque, New Mexico. In between, I continued promoting smaller concerts and regularly met with label executives from Sony, Arista, and Electra Records. Not yet 25 years old yet, I was getting paid to see concerts and meet with famous recording executives. It was truly a dream job.

Just as it was picking up steam, my concert promotion career ran into a brick wall. My company booked the rights to promote an R. Kelly tour that included Nas, Foxy Brown, Kelly Price, and Deborah Cox; it seemed like a major coup. At that moment, I was on my way to becoming the next Ron Delsner, one of the top concert promoters in the country and a legend in the industry.

We routed thirty concerts across the country and the first seven almost sold out. Unfortunately, the concert floundered and the remaining dates only sold 30 percent of available seats. Many of the final concerts were cancelled and the tour went bankrupt. The failure was definitely a low point of my life. Up until then, I had succeeded at nearly everything. The confidence and live-wire attitude that allowed me to be so successful was damaged. I did not know where to turn next.

TEAMWORK

Fortunately, one of the investors in the concert tour, Marc Sperling, was a professional stock trader. He and I had become good friends through the concert promotion business, as he had invested in most of the concerts I helped to promote. Marc knew I was a former stock broker like himself and was familiar with the markets. So when the promotion company fell apart in 1999, Marc invited me to join his trading firm. Although possessing little knowledge about how the business worked, I took to trading naturally. Where most traders would take up to six months before they started making money, I did it in half the time. Within one year, I was earning close to a six-figure income and at the end of that year, Marc had made me a manager to help coach and train other traders.

Although the work and lifestyle of a professional trader proved to be a good fit for my independent nature, profits hit a ceiling. I studied charts, talked to other traders and tried new strategies, but the improvement never came. While frustrated, I was making money, so I continued to trade, although disappointed by my inability to turn the corner. However, the necessary change came when I began training for the triathlon I had entered to honor my fallen best friend, Steven Perez.

After setting a fundraising goal, I now had to train for the race. I cut all favorite junk foods from my diet, gave up Thursday drinking nights, and adopted a grueling daily training schedule. The old lifestyle had to change forever. Once wandering into the office around 8:30 a.m. every day and heading off to happy hour at least three nights a week, I now had to follow a strict exercise regimen. For the first time, I was living a more disciplined, balanced life—and it paid off big time. The added focus allowed me to develop a complete game plan for success each day and each week.

A NEW ROUTINE

I started waking by 6:00 a.m. daily (it is even earlier now that I am a father) to be at the trading station by 7:45 a.m. During lunch, I would run, swim, or take spin classes at the gym, followed by 30 minutes of stretching. Developing a healthy routine increased my focus at the office. All my dreams for a career seemingly had come to fruition. Little did I know how much more success I could have by developing a better routine. Having to balance trading, training, and time with family and friends forced me to take control of my life. Often while working out, I would rehearse a trading strategy, allowing me to trade smarter and with more discipline upon returning to my desk. I knew that a rigorous exercise routine would make me a stronger athlete, but I did not expect the side effect—the discipline and focus from training carried over to trading.

In a typical year before doing triathlons, I would earn a comfortable six-figure income. But after I started training, profits doubled. I made more money in one month than I had ever made before. I started trading with a sharper focus with fewer emotions to distract me. Today, one of my great strengths as a trader is my ability to game-plan effectively, the result of my training. I have such little free time that I have no choice but to plan everything far in advance and stick to my plan. My new-found discipline, time management skills, and work ethic took me to another level as a trader.

When I entered my first race, the New York City Triathlon, I was able to meet my goal to raise $20,000. The Leukemia and Lymphoma Society asked me to be a team captain, mentoring 350 people and helping them raise money. Working with the LL Society opened my eyes to what is really important in life. Losing a loved one puts everything into perspective. The psychology of trading is as important as anything when it comes to making consistent profits. Many brilliant minds fail in trading because they cannot perform under pressure and eliminate emotions. Being able to take heavy losses and remain on an even keel is crucial. Having lost a best friend to cancer at 30, it is fair to say I stopped sweating the small stuff. I do not dwell on bad trades or missed opportunities. My mind is clear.

With each triathlon, my trading results continued to improve. I participated in the punishing Escape from Alcatraz triathlon, including a swim through the frigid waters of the San Francisco Bay, a bike ride through the city's steep hills, followed by a run up 400 steps of sand. "Triathletes face the risks of strong currents, treacherous 55-degree waters, and two-ton sea lions," the race website read. I endured freezing cold showers to prepare for the icy swim, which more than 20 percent of competitors do not finish in the allotted time. Next was my first Ironman, the ultimate test for an athlete. The 2.4-mile swim, 112-mile bike and 26-mile marathon provided the greatest challenge yet. A daunting task, the Ironman required almost a year of training. Having been raised my whole life to work hard and make the most of opportunities, I confidently rose to the occasion.

This new life had instilled in me a greater sense of accountability. Traders are often quick to blame a poor market or bad luck for lack of profits. The only way to make progress is to learn to look in the mirror. The market will speak if you are willing to listen, and it will tell you whether to trade aggressively or to be patient. It will tell you what stocks are in play and where they are likely headed. If you are losing in the market, it is your own fault, and that lack of accountability plagues the trading careers of many intelligent people. When you are competing in an Ironman, you learn to take responsibility for your own performance. If you do not discipline yourself to train hard and push your body to the limit, the proof will be in the pudding as you suffer through hours of excruciating pain on race day.

FINDING BALANCE

After the merger between that created T3, my role continued to expand. Most would say I am the face of T3 Live. While not the most naturally gifted trader in the firm, tireless preparation and enthusiasm makes me one of the most successful. Mentoring young traders, I try to instill the qualities of accountability and discipline needed to excel. Getting into the office by 7:15 a.m. to build the Morning Gameplan—a blueprint of what stocks are in play and where the important levels are in each—in which I underline important factors dictating how the market will trade. I perform analysis of the macro market, forecast what direction we are likely headed in, and highlight a sector to pay special attention to. We record live videos before and after the trading day, with a video before the open detailing where to look and why for that day, and one after the close to recap the day's action and where to look the next day and beyond.

While getting in early does help my own trading, as an experienced trader, I could perform this analysis in half the time. I prepare the game plan and record the videos for the firm and remote subscribers so each trader has no excuse not to succeed. Taking traders through every day on my live radio broadcast and in the chat room, I conduct meetings to take questions from and provide guidance to struggling traders. Everyone at the firm has the resources needed to take control of their trading and in turn, their life. I strive be a role model for other traders, an example of where discipline and hard work can take you.

Finally, I try to teach how to live a balanced life. I became the trader I am today because of the sense of balance I have achieved. Develop an active routine to bring health and structure to your life. Beginning in 2009, dozens of T3 traders have participated in the New York City Triathlon each July. At the same time, we also have fun. Happy hour events and dinners acknowledge individual and firm-wide success (although triathlon participants have to abstain leading up to the race). While supreme focus and discipline are important for traders, the ability to take their minds off trading, relieve stress, and enjoy the lifestyle they have created for themselves is equally important for long-term success and happiness. Nothing gives me more pleasure than seeing a trader turn the corner from survival to prosperity.

Develop an active routine to bring health and structure to your trading and your life.

At this point, I did not care about my time. Now my goal was just to finish the Ironman. I managed to reach for the salt pack, rip it open, and shove all three tablets in my mouth. The salt stung my parched throat as I lay helplessly on the asphalt. Still unable to stand, I got on my knees and began to crawl down the road, scraping my legs with every yard. More runners jogged past, but I did not care about anyone else. I was now in the middle of war between my own mind and body. Finding a half filled water bottle someone discarded, I managed to suck down the remaining fluid.

Eventually, as the salt began to take effect, I managed to stagger to my feet and head for one of the aid stations spread along the course. It represented the halfway point of the marathon. Thirteen miles remained. I could make it.

The station did not have any salt packs, but did have Lipton soup, one of the saltiest liquids you can drink. Quickly downing the soup, my desperate journey toward the finish line began. At first, I could only walk clumsily.

By mile 16, I was running again, passing friends and relatives, who had expected me to run past them forty minutes ago. The worried looks on their faces soon turned to elation as they saw me jogging down the street. I was no longer running at a fast pace, but I was going to make it. Seeing them cheer me on toward the finish made all the suffering worth it.

Crossing the finish line, a flood of emotions washed over me. Steven's laughing, smiling face immediately entered my thoughts. I wish more than anything he could have been there that day. I thought of other leukemia patients bravely fighting for their lives as he did. My struggles pale in comparison to what Steven and others stricken with cancer go through every day. Finally, I thought about my life, how hard I had worked to achieve this feeling, and how this experience had forever changed me as a person and trader.

• • •

6

Evan Lazarus
The Guru

TRADING SAVED MY LIFE

IN MY SECOND YEAR OF TRADING, THE WORLD TRADE Center towers were attacked. I watched at my office as the towers went down. I was in total disbelief, just like most of the country. My first thoughts were of deep sadness for the victims, the young men and women who were forging a life for themselves as young professionals working at the various companies that resided in the towers. I thought of their families. It was a day of great sadness for all Americans. Still, it was hard for me to stop thinking about myself.

After my dream career—sports agent extraordinaire—floundered, I found myself working at an upscale Manhattan restaurant. While filling their water glasses, I quizzed my affluent guests about their careers with hopes of finding an opportunity in finance. Most were forthcoming, offering me advice, and some even helped to get me interviews.

One interview struck me in particular. A man with whom I hit it off pretty well with offered me a chance to meet with representatives from Cantor Fitzgerald, one of the largest brokerage firms in the world. I remember visiting their offices like it was yesterday. I mean, it is hard not to remember a visit to the top of the World Trade Center. It was 1999; the company had the top floors of the building all to themselves, with one floor exclusively dedicated to their own private art museum featuring original works by Picasso and Monet, among others.

The atmosphere at Cantor Fitzgerald was exactly how I had imagined it would be. Everyone was impeccably outfitted and the offices were decorated with contemporary brilliance. The employees were confident, knowledgeable, and assured. The environment reeked of professionalism and class; if you allowed Cantor Fitzgerald to manage your money, you could trust they were going to perform due diligence to get the most out of it.

When Cantor Fitzgerald offered me a job, even at entry level, I was beside myself with joy. I had no education in finance and little knowledge of the intricacies of the market. I had landed the interview by networking as a nickel-and-diming waiter, lost and without direction in life. Now, I had the chance to work for one of the top firms of its kind in the world, at the top of one of the most iconic skyscrapers in the world. I felt confident that if I worked hard, I would quickly move on from my entry-level position and become a success-ful bond trader. My dream had come true, my prayers for a break answered. I had been lost, struggling to find direction after graduating from college, but now it seemed I was on my way.

Still, something about the corporate atmosphere gave me pause. Although I had dreamed of landing a good job, my personality just did not quite fit with the culture. I was still set on accepting the job offer, but the more I thought about it, the less excited I was about my foray into the world of finance.

Right after receiving the job offer from Cantor Fitzgerald, a friend told me about a company looking to hire stock trad-ers. I did not think much of it, but I was always interested in the market and figured that before I dove headfirst into a life of long hours and corporate posturing at Cantor, I should investigate other opportunities. I called Broadway Trading and my friend put me in touch with another friend of his, a trader named Marc Sperling.

It is fair to say my experience at Broadway fell at the oppo-site end of the spectrum from my time at Cantor. I showed up in my best suit expecting to encounter the same stuffy environment. If I had woken up and gone to my interview at Broadway in what I was wearing, I would have fit in better. Nobody was dressed up; I felt like a fool. Guys were walking around in t-shirts, shorts, flip-flops, and jeans. I felt like I had walked into a room full of computer hackers. Every-one was staring intently at their many computer monitors, methodically plugging away at their keyboards. The scene was utter chaos. Some guys sat together at worn tables, others alone at beaten up desks that looked like they had been salvaged out of a dumpster.

I told the receptionist that I was here to speak to Marc Sperling, and she soon led me to his desk in the middle of the room. As dirty fluorescent lighting flickered above me, I watched him stare intently at his screen. Marc was apparently busy because for the next two hours, he ignored my attempts at conversation and continued to trade. I remember the room was eerily quiet, not plagued by the firebrand characters whose outbursts characterized many trading floors at the time. It was like I did not even exist because nobody paid me any heed whatsoever.

That is until Marc unveiled to me a shocking revelation. "Well, what do you think?" he said. After two hours of standing behind him, sweating in my suit and tie, I was startled by his sudden desire for conversation. His interview style differed a little from the rigorous examination I had undertaken at Cantor, that was for sure. I told him the truth; I had no idea what was going on. Marc wasted no time in getting to the point. "I just made $60,000 trading stocks in the past two hours." Suddenly I was not so pissed off about having to stand around; why would he talk to me when he could be making that kind of money? As I would later understand, it was yet another great day in a generally amazing time to be a trader.

Marc's blunt sales pitch was almost all I needed to hear. Sixty thousand dollars was more than I would make in my entire first year at Cantor Fitzgerald, the company that billed itself as a mecca for someone eager to get rich exploiting the markets. I was no longer dismissing the idea of Broadway Trading. Still. I needed to hear more before I gave up such a sure-fire opportunity, one that so many would kill to have. Marc continued, explaining to me the concept of active trading. "At the beginning of the day, I generally own no stocks," Marc explained. "At the end of the day, I usually own no stocks. In between, I might buy a dozen stocks, or I might buy nothing at all. It depends on what the market's telling me to do that day." Although I began to understand a little more, it was still a blurry picture.

That night after my visit, I talked over my choices with my father. My options were simple. One, I could accept the entry-level job with Cantor Fitzgerald and have a solid career path ahead of me with a reputable firm in a beautiful office. Two, I could work with Marc Sperling at Broadway Trading on a chaotic floor in a non-descript office building, where shabby tables crammed full of computer equipment were manned by a motley crew of guys, many of whom were dressed like 13-year-old boys aspiring to become professional skateboarders.

I knew if I took the Cantor Fitzgerald job, I would be set. It was definitely the safe choice. I would instantly earn respect and admiration from others. The sense of security was a double-edged sword. I felt that although I could not go wrong by accepting the position and slowly moving up the corporate ladder, but something about it really freaked me out. I felt like Cantor Fitzgerald would be so safe and so secure that it might actually prove too methodical for me. In some twisted way, the chaotic nature of Broadway Trading appealed more to who I was as a person. I could force myself to fit into the corporate culture of Cantor Fitzgerald, but I also knew that it wasn't really me.

In the end, I made the difficult choice and there was no turning back. Big-shot bond traders do not take kindly to having their job offers turned down, especially by young kids with no experience who decide that daytrading is a more appealing choice. I was young and figured if it turned out to be a huge mistake, I could go back to the drawing board. But I was determined to make trading work for me. My dad always taught me that being a true entrepreneur was all about taking calculated risks, and I give him a lot of credit for giving me the courage to choose trading.

T3 TIP ···
Trading, like life, is all about taking calculated risks.

The opportunity with Marc Sperling at Broadway Trading seemed priceless. I had the chance to learn the craft of trading from a highly experienced trader at a time when it was hard not to make money in the market because of the technology boom. In the end, it was an opportunity I could not pass up. The sense of excitement I felt on my first day was greater than any I had ever felt, and surely eclipsed what I would have felt at Cantor Fitzgerald.

Cantor Fitzgerald's picturesque office at the top of the towers is where I would have been that September morning had I accepted their job offer. The thought was enormously upsetting, and was so poignant that I remember the feeling exactly to this day. Under the tragic circumstances of 9/11, I realized I had made a life-changing decision to become a trader.

Trading literally saved my life. In truth, trading began to change my life from my first day on the job, and continues to shape me to this day. There is nowhere I would rather be each morning than in my office analyzing stock charts for the most promising setups. While others loathe Monday mornings, I eagerly look forward to another week of action.

NOT YOUR TYPICAL TRADER

I am not your typical professional Wall Street stock trader. I did not go to an Ivy League school, did not study finance or math. I was always just an eager young kid with dreams of making it big in the world.

Getting in on the Ground Floor

I studied communications at the University of Miami with visions of one day breaking into television or radio. After graduation, I landed a job with an agent who represented some of the biggest sports broadcasters, including Pat Summerall and James Brown. When this agent offered me a job as his assistant, I jumped at the chance. The money was not good. It was barely enough to survive in Manhattan, but it seemed like a good opportunity. The road seemed paved for me to eventually become an agent myself, negotiating deals for my own star clients. I thought I had it made.

The reality of my situation did not align with my hopes for learning and growth in the industry. In my first year working for the agent, I did everything from emptying the trash to cleaning dead fish out of the aquarium. I was a glorified janitor, secretary, and indentured servant all rolled into one. If a task was deemed disgusting, tedious, or simply a waste of anyone else's time, I was the guy who did it. After a year of performing these menial tasks, I felt like I had paid my dues and deserved the chance to do more. I finally worked up the nerve to talk to my boss about taking on more important tasks.

Although my first year on the job was a major disappointment, I harbored hope that my hard work would be rewarded in time. I imagined I would ask my boss for more responsibility and he would bring me along as I continued to prove myself. It was a reasonable expectation, I thought, for a year of hard work with no complaints.

I could not have been more wrong about how my boss would respond to my request. I approached my boss and told him that while I appreciated the opportunity to work with the company, I wanted to learn more about becoming an agent. Speaking frankly about my dream and my desire for him to mentor me took a lot of courage. I finally was putting myself out there and it felt great. My boss laughed in my face. To him, I was expendable, and this mindless job was the farthest that I would go in this company. If I did not like it, I could leave and he would bring in someone else to replace me.

Anger soon turned to painful disappointment. I thought I knew what to do with my life. I thought I was in a position to realize my dream of becoming an agent. I thought life was fair and you would always be rewarded for working hard. In the end, I realized that you can only affect things that are under your control and that it is foolish to place supreme trust in others. That is why I think trading fits my personality, because I am able to get out what I put in. My hard work is rewarded directly every day, and nobody can take that away from me. Needless to say, I quit that job. I was now unemployed with no valuable work experience, uncertain about what my future would hold.

Desperate for steady income to pay my bills in New York City, I took a job as a waiter in a fancy restaurant in Manhattan. While the job involved the same manual labor that I had grown tired of at the sports agency, it was a much more pleasant environment. The management was honest with me and straightforward about my pay and what I could expect. As I began to earn more shifts, I was able to live comfortably. I remember leaving work late at night with hundreds of dollars worth of tips jammed in my pockets. Being directly rewarded for hard work feels good.

T3 TIP ···
The beauty of active trading is that you control your own destiny.
··

In trading, there is no better feeling than when you finally start to get it. When you turn the corner from survival to profitability as a trader, an irreplaceable feeling overwhelms you. There is no other business where such an overpowering feeling of self-fulfillment accompanies the initial phase of success as in trading. I began to feel some of that as my hard work at the restaurant allowed me to live well in the most expensive city in America. Although I was making money and enjoying the validation that waiting tables provided, but I knew I did not want to be a waiter for the rest of my life.

Many customers that frequented the restaurant worked on Wall Street. Stock brokers, financial analysts, and bankers came in to eat every night and I began to develop relationships with the more regular customers. I had always been interested in the stock market, but this was the first time I had ever met people who were actually making a living working on Wall Street. I took opportunities to strike up conversations with these individuals as we developed friendly relationships. Casual conversations became more serious as the customers became more comfortable. While maintaining my professionalism as a waiter, I gleaned as much advice as I could from these fountains of knowledge. As our conversations became more and more sophisticated, and my interest in finance became clear, many began to discuss with me the idea of at least coming in to interview with their firms. I was developing a network that would do nothing but open up doors for me. Without reading a book about the importance of networking, I was quickly realizing its immense value.

The best opportunity I got came in the form of the aforementioned offer from Cantor Fitzgerald. My burgeoning networking skills were paying dividends and the opportunity I got with Broadway Trading was the result of my expanded network. After my gut-wrenching decision to turn my back on Cantor Fitzgerald, it was time to get down to business trading. I was extremely fortunate to get into the market at a time when seemingly everyone was making money. My first two years in the stock market fell right in the middle of the dot-com boom. Stocks soared to dizzying heights. When it seemed stocks had climbed to unreasonably high levels and would start to pull in, they doubled. It did not take a genius—or even a human being—to make money during the tech boom of the late '90s and into the very early stages of the new millennium. All you had to do to make money was to buy a stock and then sell it after its inevitably colossal ascent.

The dot-com boom, like all booms, was a blessing and a curse for me. While I made a great deal of money during those first two years, I did not learn enough to adjust to the change in the market that was surely imminent. When the dot-com boom turned bust, I was lost. I had made money when I knew stocks were going to continue higher, latching on to their momentum for sure profits. As the market came crashing down to Earth, I looked for places to buy stocks that had pulled in. During the bust, most traders went broke, forced to the leave the business they had grown to love. I was not far from following them as my account dwindled lower and lower. I needed to make a change or risk having to start my life all over again from scratch.

TIME FOR A CHANGE

I took a trip to Las Vegas and met an older, seasoned stock trader at a party. The conversation started out as small talk, but with the market flowing through our veins and running through our brains, talk of trading took over the dialogue. The man asked me what seemed like simple question, "What is your strategy in trading the stock market?" I began to speak, but realized I did not have a good answer. During the dot-com boom, my strategy was simple and easy; buy the highest momentum stocks and ride them up. Although I was a so-called professional stock trader, this man's question stopped me in my tracks. I had no plan for making money consistently. He told me what I had come to fear after the boom was over. "Son, you're going to get busted out of the market if you don't develop a plan."

I did not take his criticism well and our conversation did not end amicably. I thought I knew what I was doing since I had been making money. When I got home from that trip, I thought more about what he said. He was right—in a changing market I needed a plan if I was going to survive as a trader. Profits were no longer being handed to me. I needed to work harder, trade smarter, and give myself an edge. I took a step back from trading in order to learn. I read every book about trading, subscribed to every magazine with information on the markets, and attended any trading or investing seminar close to me. I studied the markets closely, hoping to apply new concepts and soak up as much information as possible before making another foray into trading. I wiped my slate clean and questioned everything at a basic level. I listened to advice and studied patterns without my own personal bias and bad habits getting in the way. The post-dot-com stock market is extremely unpredictable in general, but if you remain flexible and pay attention to details, sense can be made of it all.

> *"You're going to get busted out of the
> market if you don't develop a plan."*

A PLAN FOR SUCCESS

My mantra is: "a planned trader is a profitable trader". When I started trading, I made money because it was almost impossible not to during the dot-com boom. I did not need a plan, and the bad habits I formed during that time set me back in my quest to become a consistently profitable trader. My chance conversation with the trader in Vegas was a wake-up call for me to the fact that I needed to develop a plan. Every trader has a different style, and I have been able to hone my own strategy, based around sound planning and preparation. At our firm, there are many different kinds of traders. Short-term scalpers look closely at momentum in order to capture 10 to 20 cent moves in stocks on a consistent basis. Position traders take out large positions based on a variety of factors telling them to enter, and they often experience great days and bad days. I am a swing trader, relying on my expertise in analyzing technical chart patterns to capture large moves in stocks while limiting my loss by always setting strict stop-loss points for my trade.

Trading is as simple as you make it. Many get caught up in dozens of indicators, moving averages, and formulas. Many think the more complex the strategy, the more likely it is to make money. Trading is an inexact science and must be treated as such. You cannot watch every stock out there or catch every move, but you need to identify just enough to give yourself a chance to meet a reasonable goal. As your feel gets better, goals and exposure can be increased. Trading is not gambling, it is a business—and if you approach it with a workmanlike attitude, it can be simplified.

SHARING SUCCESS

As T3Live has grown, I have become passionate about another aspect of the business: training. Because of my own struggles early in trading, training new traders is especially rewarding for me. My perspective gives the site and our program another dimension because I understand what it takes mentally and strategically to become a profitable trader. To be mildly successful, you must only master the mental side of trading while employing a simple strategy with tight stop-loss points and reasonable target prices. Next, a trader can begin performing more rigorous analysis that builds upon their successful strategy. I am a very technical swing trader, using chart patterns of longer time frames than most daytraders, along with market sentiment to identify the best trade setups. Finally able to limit losses and realize large gains on home-run trades, traders can begin to expand their scope.

Today, my office wall is covered with charts. While I do not catch every clean technical pattern, my use of filtering software and my keen eye allow me to miss out on very few moves. In training new traders, I try to use my story and my strategy as an example to give hope. The journey can be long, and it will surely be frustrating. The lows in a trader's career break most, but those who can continue to learn come out on the other side disciplined and driven to succeed. Most of my lessons in the T3 Live program center on the psychological aspect because it is the most important.

My trading strategies are successful because they are part of a plan. I am not always right, maybe not even half of the time, but when a trade works, I get paid. Knowing what you are good at gives you the confidence necessary to succeed. Knowing what you love gives you the passion to succeed. Trading truly saved my life. Living paycheck to paycheck working at the restaurant, I had no direction in life. Performing manual labor in the agent's office with no chance of growth, I felt deeply discouraged about the prospects of breaking into the industry. Trading not only prevented me from being at the top of the World Trade Center on that fateful day, it gave me a sense of purpose. Every day of my trading career, I have been excited to go to work. Not many people get to say that. I am passionate about what I do. Not everyone is so lucky. Trading saved my life because now I am in control. It is not for everyone, but if you can develop a plan for success, there is nothing like it. In my life, I have been lucky enough to find trading and turn the corner. My greatest hope, and the reason I sacrifice so much time to teach, is so that others can rescue themselves from an aimless path. After all, trading can save your life.

7

Nadav Sapeika
The Optimist

I REMEMBER SITTING IN MY DIRTY SHOEBOX OF AN apartment in the Washington Heights section of Harlem, feeling far away from anything normal or reassuring. My roommate came home and flipped on all the lights as I tried to sleep, a ritual that seemed to give him some pleasure. Having moved to New York City from Cape Town, South Africa a few months earlier at the age of 17, the assimilation was proving hard to undertake alone. It was early in the morning as I lay awake, a sea of emotions flooding my head with anxiety. I looked at my cell phone glowing in the corner of the room. There was nobody for me to call. It was the middle of the night back home in South Africa and my parents were fast asleep. I had yet to make a friend close enough to bother in the wee hours of the morning for emotional support. Far from reality, I was forced to endure another sleepless night of self-doubt. I had to think through everything on my own and pull myself through those early days in America. Instead of focusing on my problems and the uncertainty that characterized my new life, I began to urgently press on for solutions.

Fast forward to today and you would not recognize the confident entrepreneur embracing the hectic streets of New York and the inevitable challenges of life. It did not take long to revert to the cheerful optimist that I had been as a child. I had come to America to realize a dream, to transplant myself into an environment matching my ambition, and to put myself in a position to meet my goal of becoming a millionaire by age 30. It was time to get to work.

ETERNAL OPTIMIST

My wife often puzzles over my ability to remain unwaveringly optimistic in any circumstance. No matter how bad a situation may seem, my approach is always that the glass is half full. My ability to find the silver lining has shaped my life and allowed me to get where I am today. Growing up, I was always sort of the class clown, the life of party. Life was just always fun. Nothing could get me down. My friendly nature and congenial disposition led to a large group of friends and followers.

At school, all the kids played marbles. If you defeated your opponent, you got to choose several of his best marbles to keep for yourself. While everyone else was caught up playing small ball, my ever-churning brain came up with a strategy to clean up. I bought a large sack of marbles and sponsored several of my classmates in return for a cut of their winnings. Quickly, my marble collection was the envy of the student body.

It was not always smooth sailing in grade school though, and an early disappointment tested my sunny outlook. In the seventh grade, my focus strayed too far into my social life and away from my studies. I did not perform poorly in school, but when time came for placement tests to determine which high school you would attend, I just barely missed the mark. As a result of my poor performance on the final exams, I would be forced to go to a different high school than all of my close friends. I was headed for a school several miles away where I knew nobody.

Initially, I was greatly disappointed. I rued my lack of focus when the moment called for it. An important lesson was learned, and it was not long until I began to make friends and excel in my new environment. My exuberance in school was always both a curse and a blessing for teachers. The enthusiasm I brought to the classroom each day made school fun for everyone, but my energy often proved too much to handle. One note in particular my teacher sent home spoke of my tireless optimism. "Nadav is irrepressible," the note read, seemingly both a compliment and sigh of exhaustion. "Whenever anything happens to him, he always finds a way to bounce back." As it turned out, attending that high school was a blessing. I could not envision a better experience or education than what I received in my four years there. Flourishing after what seemed like a setback, I had begun to cultivate a strong will to persevere that would serve me well down the line.

BRIGHT LIGHTS, BIG CITY

At age 13, I made my first visit to New York City and the exciting, fast-paced scene immediately tickled my fancy. The culture was drastically different than the one I had grown used to in Cape Town, and it better suited my personality. Despite having barely begun my teenage years, I knew I wanted to move to America someday. Four years later, upon returning to New York for a wedding, I decided the time had come for me to make the leap.

I hoped that moving to the United States at an earlier age it would make it easier to adjust, and that an American university degree would have more clout in the job market. Always an independent person, I made all the preparations for my new life. It was something I wanted to do, so I just went for it. I prepared for and took the SAT on my own accord. I applied to colleges based on my own research, and was accepted to several before eventually choosing Yeshiva University. I did not have much of a plan beyond that, but I was handy with computers, so that seemed a good place to start. After hearing about the great opportunities to work in the booming American technology sector, I thought a computer science degree from an American university would serve me well. I thought my path to success would be clear-cut.

After graduating high school, I sprung the news on my friends and family: I was moving to New York to attend college. Friends told me I was crazy for leaving home to fly halfway around the world for college, but they did not share my thirst for challenges. I had a stated goal of becoming a millionaire by age 30 and had full belief in my ability to pull it off. After packing up one big suitcase, I waved goodbye to everything I had ever known.

The thought of leaving South Africa for America was daunting and scary, but I had proven adept at adapting to new surroundings before. Although the scale was slightly larger—a few thousand miles instead of just a few—I thought it would be a seamless and exciting transition. I did not dislike my homeland, but post-apartheid South Africa was a chaotic place. Most people who stayed in Cape Town had modest goals at best for their lives, content to stay close to home and work in a limited number of possible industries. It was never in my nature to sit idly by. Especially after my failure to make the grade in lower school, my drive was strong and ambitions were high. Possessing supreme self-confidence, I felt the only way to realize my potential was to set sail for New York City, the great city on the hill. I had visited twice in my life but hundreds of times in my dreams. Without being cliché, I held America aloft as the land of opportunity, a place where hard work and intuition would lead to a prosperous life.

Compared to Cape Town, Manhattan looked like something out of a science fiction movie. Having only gotten a brief taste of New York from my visits, once I was living there, I began to think I had bit off more than I could chew. Seventeen years old, walking down Broadway, dwarfed by massive skyscrapers and jostled by large crowds of self-interested Americans, I felt overwhelmed. I was in a city where I knew basically no one, and was now amidst a culture I did not quite understand. The excitement of the new challenge ahead lasted a few weeks, but reality soon set in. In a city filled with more than seven million people, I began to feel lost. There were no cricket stadiums or rugby fields, but rather Madison Square Garden and Yankee Stadium. Instead of the beautiful landscapes of Cape Town, there were bustling crowds in Times Square and on Wall Street. I did not know the first thing about basketball, baseball, or finance. But more glaringly, I did not know the first thing about finding my identity in this drastically different place.

FOR LOVE OF MONEY

At Yeshiva University, I began working towards a computer science major, but found its reclusive nature did not fit my affinity for human interaction. When I began college, the dot-com boom was in full swing. Stories of regular people making millions trading stocks became common tales. While at the time, I knew little about trading the stock market, it seemed clear to me that it was not too difficult to learn. The dot-com boom was a great time to be involved in stocks; I did not understand that it was not always so easy to make money as a trader. I switched my major to economics, hoping to learn some of these trading secrets. The markets had always fascinated me and I did not want to miss out on this once-in-a-lifetime opportunity to make a fortune. My cousin was a stock trader in New York at the time, so I went to him for advice on opening a brokerage account and getting involved in the stock market.

The desire to get rich got the best of me. Without a full understanding of the risks that accompany equities trading—especially during such a uniquely volatile tech boom—I opened an account. Without their knowledge, I took all the money my parents had given me for tuition and living expenses and put it in the stock market. By my junior year, after enjoying some good initial returns, I was heavily invested. Part of the money I gave to a broker to manage, and part I kept to buy and sell stocks on my own. Within a few months, I had tripled my money. The early success was the result of good fortune and only served to accelerate my eventual failure.

The dot-com boom turned bust. The money I had given to the stock broker dwindled to less than $3,000 while the positions I managed lost almost all value. A harrowing reality was upon me: I had squandered my tuition, money my parents had given me with the expectation that it get me through college. Trading served to distract me from some of the initial homesickness and loneliness I felt, and my early profits gave me hope that better days soon lay ahead. Now, I had nothing, both figuratively and literally.

As much as I dreaded the moment, I had to pick up the phone to let my parents know what I had done. I called my dad and told him exactly what happened. Naturally, he was furious. After his initial anger subsided, he calmly revealed to me what I already knew: I was truly on my own now. He could not help me pay the $25,000 per-year tuition, so if I wanted to stay in New York it was on me to finance my education and life in one of the most expensive cities in the world. My first years in a foreign country and unfamiliar culture could not have gone any worse. Despite feeling more alone than ever, I once again turned my focus to finding a solution rather than dwelling on my growing list of problems.

BY THE BOOTSTRAPS

After squandering my tuition money, there was an opportunity to learn how to survive on my own. My parents had allowed me to live comfortably by providing the money I would need through college, but now the safety net was gone. Student loans covered most of my tuition, but I was forced to earn my own money to pay for housing and living expenses.

To save money, I moved out of the dormitory and into a tiny apartment in the notoriously rough neighborhood of Washington Heights. When I was not running home from the subway stop to my apartment, I was running from cockroaches and rats in it. The apartment, if it can be called that, was about the size of my bathroom in South Africa. The living situation was certainly not ideal, but I had no other choice.

Needing a steady source of income to support myself, I got a job working as a waiter. Rather than just going through the motions to collect a paycheck, I worked hard to make the most of my time waiting tables. Being a waiter fit my personable nature very well, a fact that often led to large tips. I was always approaching my manager with suggestions and ideas. To be honest, when he promoted me to head waiter, I feel a large part of his motivation in doing so was so that I would leave him alone. No matter, my new position came with more responsibility and a bigger paycheck, two things I craved. As head waiter, the leadership qualities first demonstrated by my marble mafia began to emerge more clearly.

THE TRADE STILL CALLS

After graduating college with an economics degree, there was an itch I still felt compelled to scratch. Despite having lost my entire college tuition in the stock market, I was not ready to give up on trading. The dot-com boom was a unique time; as an uneducated trader, I was unlucky to have entered the fray at that moment in history when the bubble burst. I felt my skill set and ability to make quick decisions made me a good fit for trading. Most of all, I was still highly optimistic that with more time, I would be able to make the breakthrough. Arrogance will doom most people, but trading is a unique business where confidence is a necessary ingredient for success. I had it in abundant supply. After correcting mistakes, I knew I would make money.

Post graduation, I spent much of my free time visiting with my cousin at his trading firm. The company he was with offered me a trading position, so I learned as much as I could, preparing for the day I would "go live." As my start date approached, I called the company to ask when I should show up for my first day, and once again the rug was pulled out was from under me. "Sorry, we are no longer hiring," he said. Thanks for telling me. Finally, when I thought things were going to get easier, I was back to square one. After the post tech-boom crash, many trading firms were closing their doors to new traders as it became more difficult to make money in the new market. Unrelenting, I began contacting other firms.

Another trading firm in the building also emphasized, "We are not hiring!" But I made my way up to the office anyway. Given the chance to speak with one of the firm's partners, I boasted about my (unproven) abilities, "Just give me a chance, and I promise I will make money." I guess he believed me, because the next week he called to tell me I would be the firm's only new hire. My confidence, it seemed, had convinced them it was worth it to take a risk. Ecstatic about finally landing a trading job, I got to work backing up my audacious claim.

WATCH AND LEARN

Sean Hendelman was one of the top traders and trainers at the company. I began my career looking over his shoulder as he traded, hoping to grab morsels of useful information. He shared his strategy and served as an early trading mentor. Back in those days, training was a haphazard process, and there was no real plan for nurturing traders towards success. Trading firms threw new traders to the wolves. If they failed, they were fired and the company was not affected. If they succeeded, the company would profit. The approach carried little risk, but also did not get the most out of each trader. As I have learned in trading, no investment is worth making without significant upside potential. The process by which traders are trained needed to be overhauled.

Although I began to make money sooner than most, the road was not easy. After watching Sean for months and trying to learn as much as possible on my own, I still had little idea how to trade efficiently. The most valuable learning experiences in trading are mistakes, as long as you learn from them and do not repeat the same ones. My ability to problem solve has always been a strength, and there were plenty of failures for me to learn from in my first months of trading. Shrinking losses worked to slowly rebuild my now fragile self-confidence until I was finally able to get over the hump. But my development did not stop there. I carved out a niche as one of the top short-term scalpers at the company within my first two years. My ability to earn consistent profits allowed me to gain a strong reputation within the company.

T3 TIP

Never put yourself in a position where you have to make money trading right away. The pressure to earn will consume you and prevent you from becoming successful.

In my first year, every weekday I worked at the trading firm from 8:00 a.m. to 5:00 p.m. before heading straight to the restaurant where I waited tables until midnight. Bills still had to be paid, and because I was not making money trading early on, I was forced to continue as a waiter. Life was a grind, but I was happy to stay at the restaurant to take the pressure of my trading. Many people who enter the trading business never become profitable because they set themselves up to fail. Something I found out early on, after throwing hundreds of thousands of dollars of tuition money away in my first foray into the market, is that you cannot count on steady income from trading from the start. Many begin trading careers with unrealistic expectations. They think they will be able to get rich in a couple of months, pay for a posh apartment in Manhattan and "pop bottles" at the hottest new clubs. When things do not go as expected, their trading suffers because panic and stress prove debilitating. Needing to make money to get by, traders succumb to the pressure and are forced out of the business. Upon starting my trading career, I knew success was not guaranteed. By living in a cheap apartment and working nights as a waiter, I did not put myself under pressure to pay the bills with trading profits. I could come to work each day with a clear head knowing I would have a roof over my head and money to feed myself. However much time it took me to finally make consistent profits, it did not matter. Waiting tables actually served to straighten me out after a tough day trading. Performing manual labor and learning the value of money, I had greater perspective each day. Staying busy prevented doubt from creeping in.

Naturally, my parents were horrified when I told them I was getting back into the stock market. My girlfriend was worried I was gambling with my future. Their concerns were justified, given how much I had gotten hurt before. But having learned my lesson, I was not going to lose like that again. I just had a feeling that trading was what I was meant to do. Still, I wanted to offer my girlfriend (now my wife) the stability she and her family wanted and deserved.

TURNING A CORNER

I had begun to make enough money trading to pay the bills and allow me to quit my job as head waiter of the restaurant. While continuing to trade stocks during the day, at night I would attend law school at Rutgers University. If in four years I could not make a good living in the stock market, I decided that I would become a lawyer. Going to law school seemed like a great fall-back option, but my heart was still set on trading. Most people thought I was crazy for trying to get a law degree while working a full-time job. I did not see a problem. Besides, I had been working nights waiting tables for the past several years.

Trading all day and then going to law school at night might seem difficult, but I actually liked the variety it gave me each day. After a full day of trading, going to law school was a change of pace that helped relieve stress. Trading and law are very different disciplines, and the combination helped me become a well-rounded person. Perhaps the most important lesson I learned in law school was to trust myself. Unlike other students, I did not have time to study endlessly, so I had to rely on my ability to grasp and interpret class material quickly. I had to be efficient. Any time I was in the classroom or studying the material, I had to be extremely focused to get the most out of the limited number of hours in a day. Instead of memorizing information, I learned to understand and apply the material to answer questions. I was never the best student in the class, but, despite my limited time for study, I was not far off.

It did not take long for me to realize that I never wanted to practice law. Within two years, I started earning good money trading consistently. Wanting to finish what I started, I stuck it out to get my law degree. My knowledge of law has been a great asset. While my wife and family were not thrilled with my decision to continue trading full-time, they were beginning to understand my passion. I remember sitting down with my wife, probably sounding like a stubborn addict, explaining to her my feelings. "I have to trade."

CONSISTENCY

The other traders at my first trading job used to always joke with me about my painstaking consistency. While others' profit-and-loss fluctuated greatly, my returns were so consistent on a day-to-day basis that it seemed unnatural. Each day, I would trade the same stocks using the same methodical scalping method, and within an hour would make around $1,100. No matter if the market rallied in the afternoon or there was another stock market crash, I would leave the office every day with close to the same amount of money. My focus was on developing a consistent routine and not giving back profits. I liked taking home a sizable paycheck each month and was willing to forgo the huge month so long as I never felt the dismay of a losing one. My trading style reflects this risk-averse attitude.

As I became a better trader, partners at the firm installed me as one of the head trainers. My ability to work with people and my disciplined approach—along with my passion for trading—allowed teaching the craft to come naturally. Just as I had become head waiter because of my personable nature, I began to distinguish myself as a teacher as well. My leadership qualities became apparent to those at the trading company and my role continued to grow. Instead of continuing to train new traders one-on-one in a disorganized manner, I recommended bringing in groups of traders at once and training them together. The partners of the firm were hesitant to change the status quo. In fact, I had many ideas that met resistance from management. Trading was good, but as a budding entrepreneur, I looked for ways to expand my business.

PARTNERSHIP

An older trader impressed by both my consistent trading and successful training methods approached me about forming a new company. It was the first offer of its kind, so I jumped at the chance. At the time, I did not know a whole lot about running a small business or how to operate a business partnership. It turned out to be a very one-sided arrangement. I figured in time, my ownership stake would grow and my workload would decrease. However, the company floundered, and I was discouraged over my failure.

What I would soon learn is that to run a successful business, you need to have a solid business plan and strong partnership. In my first partnership, I did the majority of the work running the administrative side and training traders. While I did most of the work, I held a much smaller portion of the ownership. Still, I knew I had what it took to run a successful trading firm, training program, and small business. Another opportunity came along. Sean Hendelman, my former mentor and trading colleague, approached me about starting a firm. This time, I had a much better feeling.

Sean and I had remained close since his days as my trainer, so we decided to start our own firm designed to maximize his entrepreneurial skill and incorporate my training program. We had a detailed plan, a strong bond of trust, and the work ethic to get it done.

At the new company, Nexis Capital, our first class of traders numbered less than a dozen, but within a year our ranks swelled to 85 as new traders caught on to our disciplined approach. New traders were able to learn from and relate to each other's experiences. Teaching gave me great satisfaction. Most of our traders came in with no background in the business, and that is how I preferred it. By wiping their slates clean, I was able to mold traders not limited by bad habits or preconceived notions. Since Nexis merged with

Sperling Enterprises, I have been able to train even more traders through T3 Live.

There have been many times when I have questioned my career choice. Many are correct in packing it in when the going gets tough. The grind is not for everyone. For me, though, trading has always been sort of a fun challenge, an oversized rubix cube that takes a great deal of work and analytical skill to solve.

Most people who get into trading are looking for the easy buck. After working years in another job, receiving little pay for working hard doing something they loathe, individuals see trading as the house on the hill, a dream job that will immediately yield huge profits working short hours. To be honest, I saw it that way in the beginning, too. Only when I approached trading as a business did I start to achieve success. Individuals with unrealistic expectations fail before they make their first trade. I have seen so many smart people and Ivy League honor students fall flat on their faces. Intelligence is useless at the trading desk if the mindset is not right. The most successful approach their trading like am small business; they see themselves as entrepreneurs willing to do what it takes to find something that works.

The important thing—and the hardest thing for most people—is getting out of bed the day after another stinging loss and getting excited to try it again. Every morning, I am excited to meet the challenge. Never too high when times are good or too low when losses begin to mount, the ability to stay on an even keel has allowed me to survive this stressful business. For example, in 2008 as the market crashed, our firm had its best year ever, but I did not get caught up. I knew the action would slow, as it did a couple of months into 2009. I just kept grinding it out. Trading is cyclical and there are many variables in play. You have to be the constant that makes the equation work.

At this stage of my career, I have transitioned into a more supervisory role with the T3 Trading Group. I oversee and manage all trading operations while imparting my trading knowledge in a more formal setting.

My life has certainly been a roller-coaster. I was forced to leave all my best friends in grade school. Feelings of extreme loneliness and homesickness in America did not make me lose faith in my future. I lost six figures of college tuition money within 18 months of leaving South Africa trying to play the market, and was forced to work day and night to make ends meet. In what I thought would be my road into trading, I was handed a pink slip before my first day. It took me months to make a single cent trading, but I remained confident that a breakthrough would come. My first trading partnership failed miserably. After becoming a partner in a firm, several major computer glitches caused me and my firm to lose a large portion of profits, but I always looked for solutions. One reason my trainees have enjoyed such a high success rate in the industry is because they learn not only my disciplined approach, but they come to share my passion for trading. While being able to make sound decisions quickly is important for a trader, the ability to stay supremely confident and positive about the journey is exponentially more. Almost 8,000 miles from where I grew up, one thing is for sure: I have come a long way.

Part II
||||||||||||||||||||||||||||||

Lessons

• • •

8

Lessons from Sean

WHILE MANY PEOPLE STATE A DESIRE TO BE AN entrepreneur, few truly comprehend the meaning of that word. The fact of the matter is that the majority of small businesses fail within the first year, and it is not because they are run poorly. Being an entrepreneur simply requires a certain skill-set.

Trading is the most entrepreneurial business in the world. Early on in my career, I realized I was ill-suited for the corporate world because I felt strangled. A trader is one part control freak and one part adrenaline junkie, and the best traders are always calculated. The same qualities that make someone a good entrepreneur make them a good trader.

The reason I was so attracted to trading despite having a great job at Greenwich Capital Markets out of college was because I thought it would be the perfect platform for me to exercise my entrepreneurial skills. Over the course of several years, several jobs, several partnerships, several successes, and several failures, I continued to learn what it meant to truly be a good entrepreneur. People along the way taught me valuable lessons. Experiences demonstrated what did and did not work for me. I always learned more from mistakes and failures than from successes. The most important factor, though, was me. I do not pretend to be the smartest man in the world, but I do not accept failure. There is no such thing as a good loser. In my opinion, a good loser is simply a loser. I have been self-motivated to achieve success, not driven by money or anything else. No matter what obstacles have arisen, I have found a way to conquer each challenge and continue moving forward.

BE PROACTIVE

The most important quality of an entrepreneur and a trader is that they are proactive. Without the go-getter mentality, things just do not get done. There are plenty of successful people in the world who do not possess this quality. There are jobs in which people can simply put their head down and do what they are told, and many prefer it that way. But to be an entrepreneur, you can not wait for someone else to tell you what to do. You have to go out and take what you want. A "take no prisoners" approach can lead to limitless success if combined with a sound business plan and thorough preparation.

Learn

The first lessons any child learns are from his parents. For me, these lessons in being proactive started at an early age. Nothing was ever given to me by my parents. Whether it was searching for a job or deciding what to study, my parents did nothing more than nudge me in the right direction. They provided guidance and support, but when it came to getting things done, I was on my own. Any bashful part of my personality was quickly erased. The way my parents "managed" me not only cultivated a proactive mentality, but also taught a valuable lesson in managing people. The only way to inspire confidence and results in others—kids, employees, etc.—is to empower them to take the mantle.

Sports also can serve as a powerful teaching tool for young people. My parents also believed in the power of athletics to reinforce good habits and a competitive spirit. Growing up, I played tennis and hockey at a high level, and if you ask me, I still can! My father was no Earl Woods, and I certainly am not Tiger, but he did push me to be the best that I could. Doing things half-heartedly leads to bad habits, and success is all about building good ones. Especially with tennis, I trained hard to maximize my athletic gifts. Hitting extra shots each day, running sprints at the end of a lesson, and studying my approach helped me to become a good player and feel a sense of pride and accomplishment.

T3 TIP ···
Many former athletes are successful traders because the qualities of discipline and execution under pressure carry over.

Apply

In college and early in my career, I continued to apply these lessons. My focus was always on moving forward. When I struck out in my initial job search and returned home to teach tennis lessons as I had done in high school, I truly felt like I had taken a step back. It was not a good feeling. Mentally, however, I tried my hardest not to approach it that way. Tennis lessons were a networking opportunity. Be proactive, I thought, and good things will come. Sure enough, one conversation led to another and next thing I knew I was working at Greenwich, one of the largest mortgage-backed securities players in the world at that time. I did not wait for a job to come to me; I engaged each person I met to see if they might hold the key to a powerful opportunity. I was probably a little bit annoying. These people were coming out to the country club to forget about their jobs, to escape talk of work and career, but I insisted on bringing them back to it. It was the only way for me to continue moving forward, to make the most out of where I was.

A proactive approach not only led me into a great job, it allowed me to excel at GCM. I gained a reputation for getting things done, and for achieving results, something bosses love to see. I was not a brown-noser or a suck-up; I let my work speak for itself. When I did achieve something positive, though, I was not shy in making sure my superiors knew about it. I gained more responsibility with each passing week, and for me, responsibility equals opportunity. Always moving forward, never standing still. Yes, I had a good job and could keep my job while doing less work, but I was not content with where I was. If you are not taking a step forward, you are taking one back. On the advice of my mentor and boss, Bill Gallagher, I moved to the trading floor to further my career. Soon I realized, however, that my ambition had outgrown my surroundings, and although I could continue to move

> *If you are not taking a step forward, you are taking one back.*

up in the company, I was impatient. I needed to stretch my legs. I felt prepared to go out and achieve success in a less established and secure setting. Although trading involves a certain degree of uncertainty, I felt the utmost confidence that I would find my way.

After early struggles, I became a top trader at my company. I have talked about being proactive in terms of finding a job, improving my tennis stroke, and getting work done within a corporate environment, but any conversation about the merits of being proactive could start and end with trading. In trading, you get out what you put in. I have seen so many brilliant people fail or not reach their potential as traders because they did not grasp the value of being proactive. Trading is not easy. You can learn all the technical analysis you want, use dozens of complicated indicators, and write a complete list of trading rules, but until you actually get in to the trenches and experience the emotional roller coaster, you do not know anything.

Improve

Success is born from how well you learn from mistakes and how well you handle adversity. You must be proactive in identifying what is holding you back and how you can fix it. You must be proactive in seeking out advice from experienced traders and incorporating their lessons into your own trading. A trade itself needs to be proactive rather than reactive. You have to be one step ahead of the action. If you are a reactionary trader, stocks will make their moves before you are ready to pull the trigger, and you will get hurt when the trade snaps back against you.

Especially during the early days in trading, there was not a lot of formal training for new traders. Any money you made was a bonus for the company. They were content to let the cream rise to the top and let the pretenders fall to the way-side. The ones who made it were the ones who took an active interest in their own trading. That meant hounding the best traders to see what they were doing. That meant building relationships with the guys putting up the five and six figure days so that they wanted to help you. That meant picking their brains to see not only what their strategies were, but what aspects of their personality and mental approach allowed them to deal with the inevitable ups and downs. I did all those things, and the result was an efficient approach with consistent results.

T3 TIP ···
Understanding the mentality of a good trader is much more important than learning his strategies.

Always moving forward, never standing still. I was making a good living as a trader, but I wanted to continue advancing myself. By that point, I had amassed a significant amount of capital and achieved a strong reputation as a trader, so the next logical step in my mind was starting my own trading company.

Starting my own company was always a dream. I would come up with a rock-solid business plan, find a few reliable and trustworthy partners, and would soon be doing something I loved on my own terms. Well, I soon found out it is not quite that easy. Trading was definitely something I enjoyed and was good at, but owning a company with other people creates a lot of friction. At that point in my life, I was still fairly young and naïve about what to expect from other people. Once again, as was the case at GCM, I felt constricted, limited by my lack of trust and belief in other people. Also, I was interested in growing into more lucrative arenas.

Expand

I had heard about high-frequency, automated trading and was very interested in the fast-developing industry. Humans have inevitable limitations, but computer trading has very few. Over the course of the last decade, the markets have seen a dramatic shift towards a more electronic marketplace. It was clear to me the future of trading was in the high-frequency space, so it was time to once again learn everything I could in order to take a step forward. That step turned out to be a giant leap. I performed countless hours of research, interviewed as many people as I could about automated trading strategies, and worked to understand what it would take to start my own technology-oriented trading business. The business was born, and within months would become a highly profitable, multi-strategy trading machine.

In the same way, T3 Live represents a byproduct of my pro-active mindset. At Nexis Capital, we boasted a higher-than-average retention rate for new traders. Responsible for that rate was our dynamic and effective training program. As a young trader, I felt firms were missing out on a great opportunity by not committing more resources to training their traders. Yes, they would always profit from volume, but they were forgoing significant profits by not helping traders maximize their potential. While only the most proactive traders survived in the early days, at Nexis, we recognized the opportunities that would accompany a more comprehensive training program.

At the same time we recognized the effectiveness of our program, we realized a significant opportunity also existed in broadening the scope of our program. A void still existed for traders, both remote and for other firms, in training and continuing education. T3Live.com was built first as a way for us to communicate and share all training and analysis with satellite trading offices. We wanted to share the analysis of our top traders in the New York office with all other traders in order to help them become more productive and efficient. Eventually, outsiders heard about this program we had developed and began clamoring for access to T3 Remote (or what was originally called Nexis Remote Training, or NRT). We opened up T3 Live to the retail community, and the feedback has been overwhelmingly positive. The evolution of T3 Live has followed along much like the evolution of the Internet. A group of people wanted a way to more efficiently and effectively share information and interact, and the idea evolved into a broad-reaching tool for anyone to access a limitless sea of useful information.

I was proactive in leveraging our training program into T3 Live. Investing in the programming and infrastructure it would take to build, maintain, and host a website in-house, the website began to quickly grow its grassroots subscriber base. Traders around the country began to hear about our service and were immediately intrigued. T3 Live offers traders the ability to listen and follow experienced professional traders live as well as through on-demand market analysis videos. Just as I had worked to pick the brains of the successful traders at my first trading job, I had created the opportunity for anyone to pick the brains of our most successful T3 traders. The website has continued to grow and evolve. Subscriber loyalty is tremendous because of the value-added service we provide to traders.

The lesson from all of this is that if you are proactive and diligent, anything is possible. When I was out on those tennis courts during hot summer days, sure, I got discouraged. Yes, I have had many moments of doubt during my career, doubts about whether I would ever achieve success, whether I had made the right decisions along the way. Ultimately, however, I did not let those doubts distract me from my work. I remained proactive; I never settled for where I was because I realized there was always room for me to move forward. I could easily still be at GCM, contently working my way up the corporate ladder. I could easily still be exclusively a manual trader, making good money doing something exciting and dynamic. I could still be managing client money in a traditional hedge fund, using my quantitative skills to deliver solid returns to investors. But if I had stopped moving forward and being proactive at any stage, I would have been cheating myself. The value

The value of change should never be underestimated and its inevitability cannot be ignored.

of change should never be underestimated and its inevitability cannot be ignored. Circumstances and goals will always change, but the important thing is that you always push forward to learn the necessary lessons for success. A passion for entrepreneurship burns inside of me that has become so engrained in my personality that is has become impossible to simply stand still.

T3 is a one-of-a-kind company, the culmination of several successes and failures throughout my career. We deliver trading services to anyone who seeks to explore opportunities in the financial markets. Still, the reason we remain on the forefront of the trading world is because we are always pushing the envelope. The next opportunity is just around the corner, and if we are not proactive in taking advantage of it, someone else will. For you the trader, the businessman, or the person, you must embrace that reality if you want to be the best version of yourself. An entrepreneur's sense of self-actualization upon achieving what they set out to do is a truly amazing and unique feeling. No matter what you are doing now or picture yourself doing in ten years, be proactive and good things will come. If you continue to work hard and take steps forward, you will achieve success. Take pride in the process and the results will soon follow.

The following are the most important lessons I have learned over the course of my journey. After years of searching, I have finally found a group of people with diverse and complimentary talents whom I can trust fully, and built a complete company whose product I whole-heartedly believe in.

LEADERSHIP

While hard work has been a large component of my success, it would clearly have been impossible to achieve what I have alone. My ability to surround myself with highly intelligent and hard-working people, and to get the best out of those people, has largely driven my success.

As an individual, being proactive is an important ingredient for success. When you become the leader of a company or a group of people, however, the ability to manage those people effectively becomes the most important skill. While there are certainly qualities that universally define good leaders, each person has their own style and personality to incorporate into how they manage and interact with people. My approach to dealing with people is simple: always listen, treat people with fairness, and empower others to take the reins. To be successful, you must surround yourself with the right people and allow them to make you and your business better. Effectively dealing with people has direct applications to trading, as the best traders are those who continue to learn from the people around them.

The Right People

The first, and most important, aspect of this formula is surrounding yourself with the right people. I have been fortunate to be surrounded by good people for most of my life. As I get older, I look for the same qualities in the people I work with as the people who raised me and who I grew up with. At each step in my journey, there have been trustworthy and smart people whom I have worked with and learned a tremendous amount from. My relationships have evolved as I have gotten older, but I still try to learn as much as possible from people.

As a manual trader, it is pretty much every man for himself. The only way to get ahead is to establish relationships with the most successful traders. Early on in my trading career, I latched onto the best and brightest trading minds I could find. The value of surrounding myself with good traders was immeasurable. When I first started, I was brash and overconfident. Hearing about all the people making fortunes trading at the time, I figured it was easy and I would enjoy instant success. I only got over the hump once I started to listen to other people. There is always someone who knows more than you, and it is important to understand that to keep moving forward. Trading is a difficult and dynamic business, and you need all the help you can get.

Moving forward for me meant starting my own firm. In a business partnership—especially a trading partnership—it is important to team with people you trust. In my first partnership, I did not have those people. At that time I was naïve; I thought others would have my best interests at heart as well as their own. I do not regret the way things turned out because I learned valuable lessons about how to do business. Moving forward, I would place a particular emphasis on finding people I can trust. When the time came to start my next company, I turned to a friend and former trading pupil, Nadav Sapeika. I had mentored him in my short-term trading style and we had developed a close friendship and working relationship. We teamed up to create Nexis Capital, the company that would eventually merge with Sperling Enterprises to form T3. Nadav and I together created the training program that would become T3 Live.

When the time came to move into the high-frequency trading arena, there was again a need to surround myself with good people. In high-frequency trading, there are two challenges in creating profitable trading systems—coming up with the strategies, and programming them. Both aspects of automated trading are barriers to entry, and I needed to master both of them to stay ahead of the game. Most of my strategies were similar to ones I used as a trader, tweaked and perfected by a computer's precise and decisive stroke. I studied what worked in the markets and incorporated characteristics of different trading styles into my black boxes. The most difficult part would be finding the brightest programmers, people who could correctly program the strategies while remaining loyal to me. Again, I was fortunate to find brilliant people to help bring my vision to reality.

Open Lines of Communication

People remain loyal to a company when they are treated fairly and feel like their ideas are being taken to heart. In addition to surrounding myself with good people, I have always understood what it is to be a good listener. Effective communication is one of the greatest challenges in the workplace and one of the most difficult balancing acts for a manager. People become disillusioned and unproductive when they feel they are not being heard. When

Being an effective leader means surrounding yourself with good people, being a good listener, treating people with fairness, and empowering others.

individuals feel like they are being treated fairly and managers are truly listening to their ideas and concerns, they become productive and happy. Another effective aspect of communication is telling people when they have not met expectations. While incorporating others' ideas and giving positive feedback are important principles, they are only credible if also surrounded by moments of constructive criticism. Create an open environment where employees and partners feel comfortable communicating. If lines of communication are open, ideas will be expressed more readily, more work will get done, and standards will be clear.

AUTOMATED HIGH-FREQUENCY TRADING

Today's version of the stock market is very different than the one that existed at the beginning of my career. The market today has become characterized by lightning fast execution speeds, tiny spreads and high volatility. The change has been primarily brought about by the rise of high-frequency (or black box) trading. Computer trading now accounts for nearly 70 percent of market volume. Most HFT strategies are short-term, relying on speed to take advantage of market inefficiencies. The increased liquidity brought about by automated trading is the best thing that ever happened to the markets, retail investors, and even the majority of manual traders. A byproduct of the technology arms race is that the markets have become highly efficient. If you understand what will continue to work in the new era, you stand to gain more than ever before.

Black box trading spans all different types of strategies. Computers are programmed to trade based on an endless set of criteria. You can build a black box strategy for anything.

There are black boxes for low-risk value investing, technical analysis-driven swing trading, and short-term scalp trading. The only qualifier is that a computer makes the trades automatically. In the beginning, traders were drawn to automated trading because it eliminated the much vaunted psychological challenges traders faced on a daily basis. Many traders have sound strategies that work in a vacuum, but when it came time to execute, they could often not handle the swings or would lose focus during trading. With a computer, the strategy trades itself without hesitation or anxiety. Whether executing a short-, medium- or long-term strategy, computers can ensure the cleanest entries and exits.

Slippage

The term slippage refers to the difference in the expected price of a trade and the price a trade actually executes, a very important concept for traders in a crowded marketplace. When making hundreds of trades a day and/or trading large amounts of stock, minimizing slippage can be the difference between winning and losing. If you are executing a trade and experience slippage of ten cents with 10,000 shares on both the entry and exit, that is $2,000 dollars needlessly slipping out of your pocket! Slippage occurs most often during volatile periods where bids and offers may change quickly. Precise entries and exits separate the good traders from the great traders. The goal of high-frequency trading is to eliminate that slippage in trades by making execution instantaneous. Furthermore, the most consistent and profitable strategies are those that take advantage of slippage in the market as their primary strategy, leveraging extensive technology infrastructure and connectivity to beat everyone else to the punch.

Style

As a manual trader, my style was all about limiting risk and fast execution. When I started my first black box, I wanted to focus on building an algorithm that would mimic that consistent approach. High-frequency trading appealed to me because it matched my style as a trader. I also did a great deal of research and reading—testing strategies and incorporating ones that worked into my boxes while scrapping the ones that did not. At T3, I operate 30 to 50 strategies each day depending on the market, and almost all are short-term, order-based strategies that rarely ever see a losing day. Programmers tweak strategies based on performance metrics and analytics, maintaining a fluid approach to conquering an ever-changing market. On a daily basis, I adjust aggression levels based on the success of a particular strategy. The most common time for me to adjust aggression levels is during the first and last hour of trading. If the boxes are working well, I will put the pedal to the metal; if they are not performing as well, then I will tug on the reins.

Changing Markets

The complexion of the markets has changed significantly as a result of high-frequency trading. The proportion of trades the NYSE handles has shrunk from 80 percent in 2005 to 40 percent today, and that figure continues to fall. The iconic floor of the NYSE holds much less significance than it used to as ECNs and other exchanges have grown in popularity because of high-frequency trading demands. T3Live's technology division currently houses a server at the NASDAQ co-location facility in Carteret, New Jersey to ensure fast and reliable execution. High-frequency firms invest heavily in technology infrastructure because it dictates speed, consistency, and level of success.

There are many players in the high-frequency trading game. Institutions like endowments and pension funds conduct high-frequency trading activities to balance orders and reduce slippage; banks trade their own capital; large hedge funds like Renaissance Technologies' Medallion Fund employ high-frequency strategies; and smaller start-up firms like T3 trade private capital. The Medallion Fund specifically was one of the first to use a predominantly high-frequency algorithm strategy, and is regarded as one of the most successful hedge funds on the planet, averaging 35 percent returns from 1989 to 2009. The field will definitely continue to grow.

The potential risks of a highly computerized stock market are greatly exaggerated. The range of high-frequency trading strategies are so diverse that it is nearly impossible that a black box-driven market collapse could ever occur, and uptick regulations have been put in place to prevent such a meltdown from occurring. Black boxes do not create volatility; they generally smooth out the peaks and valleys. When volatility occurs, high-frequency trading strategies make money by restoring order. In reality, high-frequency trading generates profits largely because it is a service provider— a provider of liquidity. In a now-decentralized market, the need exists for an efficient and cost-effective way to match buyers and sellers. High-frequency trading provides that service. Since the increase in automation, both spreads and fees have decreased dramatically for retail investors. Traders are now afforded the luxury of high liquidity along with precise and near instantaneous execution.

High-frequency is the wave of the future in trading. The increased automation has created an environment where the most savvy and sophisticated traders can succeed like never before. When I say sophisticated, I do not mean the most intelligent or the person using the most advanced indicators. I mean the individuals who have the greatest understanding and awareness of the current landscape, the individuals who best understand their own strengths and limitations. Firms specializing in high-frequency trading are now also reducing barriers to entry for individuals into the automated trading realm. Many companies, T3 included, now offer the full range of technology services to individual accounts who want to create and operate an automated strategy. From implementation and programming of the strategy to the use of data servers for instantaneous execution, to dynamic performance analytics, anyone can utilize our assets to enter the high-frequency trading realm.

9

Lessons from Marc

TRADERS ARE UNIQUE ANIMALS. AS A TRADER, YOU DO not have the luxury of a guaranteed salary. You do not have the structure of a corporate job. The pressure to perform at the top of your game exists every single day. You can not afford to have off days. There are plenty of traders who can have big days or big months, even good years, but only a small percentage of those people achieve success in the long run. I have distinguished myself in the trading world through my ability to achieve results year after year. Based on my experience, the greatest lesson I can teach is how to achieve longevity in trading. By no means was it a smooth ride, and in no way did it always come naturally to me. Through years of hard work and self-evaluation, I have honed my technique and hardened my psyche. In the end, though, it all boils down to how well you know yourself.

Relatively speaking, my career got off to a flying start. There is a definite learning curve in trading, and anyone who tells you otherwise is lying. My career began during the infamous tech boom, so I made money fairly early on. After losing money my first seven weeks on the job, I turned the corner to profitability and there was no looking back. My early success was a double-edged sword. The fact that I made good money from the start ensured that I was never burdened by having to dig out of a huge hole, but the money was fool's gold. The relative ease of making money at that time in the market created bad habits. In my head, I thought it would always be so easy. I never shorted stock or even fathomed that stocks would go down for any prolonged period of time. All I would do was buy dips and watch as stocks continued to climb higher. I was good at what I did, but ultimately I was a one-dimensional trader.

NEVER STOP LEARNING

Basically, I did not learn a lot about trading because I did not have to. I never really put in the time at the beginning to build the complete foundation, to educate myself. I was able to make money and avoid big losses because the market always went up. As a young man achieving great success, I was naïve to how unsustainable the market was. In retrospect, of course the market could not continue to go up. The tech bubble would inevitably burst at some point, but my focus was on the here and now. Unfortunately, like many traders of that era, I had to learn my lesson the hard way.

The world is full of people who are looking for the quick and easy buck. "Bubbles" are inevitable phenomena, the byproduct of greed and recklessness. Life and business are cyclical. Good times are followed by more difficult ones. When times are tough, it is an opportunity for people and businesses to retrench. Families save more and spend less. Individuals burned by risky investments become more risk-averse. Companies trim the fat and become more efficient and dynamic. Governments loosen the strings to create jobs. Slowly things begin to recover. In the end, things get better and people again start to live beyond their means and search for the next great opportunity to get rich in a day. Things are never as good or as bad as they seem. The next upturn or downturn is right around the corner.

The tech boom and the prolonged bull market of the late '90s made trading all the rage, the latest way to get rich. Online and discount brokerages drew the retail public into the stock market and there was a snowballing effect. It was never like that for me, though. From the first day I started trading, it was my passion. Even when things took a turn for the worse, my commitment to the business never wavered. In 2001, there was a mass exodus from professional daytrading. The suckers were flushed out and only the most sophisticated and passionate traders were left to navigate the barren landscape. The ocean had dried up, but the journey for me had just started.

The fact that I had never built the foundation as a trader probably cost me eight figures during the shakeout of the tech boom. You can do the math, but needless to say, I lost a good chunk of money. My bad habits and one-dimensional approach caught up to me. Each day I was dumb-founded as the market continued to go down. I had always brushed off risk because I knew I could recover any loss in a matter of minutes. As the losses mounted, my confidence became increasingly fragile. In my first two-and-a-half years, I could count net losing days on two hands. I built myself up with an emphasis on being green every day, and little by little I became a name in the industry. I built a base of capital that was indestructible and with it grew my sense of self-confidence. Beyond the money, my greatest loss was the swagger that defined me as a trader.

Just as the hard times give companies a chance to reexamine operations and cut costs, the lull in the markets gave me a chance to build that foundation I never had. I learned the intricacies of technical analysis and how to interpret charts. I became versatile instead of one-dimensional. I began to more closely examine many of the psychological barriers that prevent traders from reaching their full potential. Most importantly, I learned the need for active risk management. Over the course of the next few years, I made a good living despite lower volatility and liquidity in the markets. Trading is no pipe dream; it is a job and a business. The opportunists who made a quick buck during the boom only got to taste the whipped cream on top of the sundae. They only got to see the tip of the iceberg. There were a lot of big eyes and not enough heart. The markets would improve and the floodgates would reopen, and the ones who would make the real money during that time would be the ones who put in the time to truly learn about themselves and what would make them successful in the market.

CONFIDENCE

In my experience, the best traders are those individuals who are supremely confident and know themselves extremely well. Obviously there is more to being a great trader, but once you have reached a certain level of experience, those qualities differentiate the contenders and pretenders.

Being truly confident is not as easy as it sounds. There is a big difference between thinking you are confident and being confident. Most people, to a certain degree, believe they are confident. Especially in trading, there are a lot of big shots who think they are God's gift to the world, but the moment they are faced with adversity, that false confidence is irreparably damaged. In some ways, confidence is something that you are born with or cultivated at a young age. Even more-so, however, confidence is something that is built through experience.

There is a lot that goes into being truly confident. Confident people get what they want, whether it be the girl, the job, or the stock. They are driven and decisive when the moment calls for it. Think to yourself, who are the most confident people in the world? What comes to mind for me are the most successful professional athletes and businessmen in the world. There are plenty of basketball players that can shoot as well as Michael Jordan. There are golfers who hit the ball farther and straighter than Tiger Woods. Yes, both Tiger and Michael put in the work to learn the game and hone their technique, but that is not what makes them great. They are special because of their unwavering confidence and fierce competitive drive. Donald Trump is not the smartest guy in the room and has gone bankrupt several times, but at each turn he is decisive in building his brand and growing his empire.

Although some are predisposed to have more confident personalities, most have to work to build it. No matter how you are as a person, you still have to build yourself up as a trader. For me, that experience happened in two stages. You have to go from zero to positive, and then from positive to lucrative. I started from nothing to become a confident money-making machine. At the beginning of my career, I put an emphasis on being positive each and every day. Whether it be $50 or $500, I was satisfied only if I ended the day positive. Each positive began to add up, and my confidence grew gradually along with my trading account. During the tech boom, I knew I could pull money out of that raging bull market each and every day. If I had a bad trade, I knew I would make it back in the next one. In retrospect, there was definitely a chink in the armor though. The market went down and took me with it. I was back to square one as a trader. I had to start the process over again. I was back at zero and had to regain the confidence that I could make money every day. For a period I was unsure of myself, but I remained confident that I would learn how to conquer the new market.

T3 TIP ....

You build confidence as a young trader by being consistent, not swinging for the fences.

A large part of being confident is being able to overcome adversity. If you prove to yourself you can deal with misfortune, you will put yourself in a position to excel at the next opportunity. Adversity can either set you back or become motivation, and a confident individual uses it as fuel. Let's revisit the athlete analogy. Michael Jordan's rise to stardom was not all smooth sailing. During his Hall of Fame induction speech, Jordan made it a point of highlighting moments in his life where he was slighted by other people. To most, Jordan came off as arrogant and cheap, taking one final opportunity on a grand stage to prove he was the ultimate alpha male. To me, it was a fierce competitor revealing priceless insights into what made him great. When he was cut from his high school varsity team as a sophomore, he worked harder than anyone else to prove he belonged on the team. When he came up short in his quest for a title at the beginning of his career, he worked on ways to make his teammates better. Each time he was presented with a challenge, he confidently overcame it.

Both professional sports and professional trading demand that you are always on top of the game. There is no time to rest on your laurels. The best in the business are the greatest competitors, the ones who are always trying to take their game to the next level. When I was younger, it would always bother me if someone else had a bigger day than me. I felt I was the best and did not see any reason why I should not have the biggest gains each and every day. In no way was my competitive nature toxic—I wanted everyone to do well—but seeing other people do better always irked me in a way. There was never a sense of entitlement, but at all times I had the utmost confidence that I would make the most money.

SELF-KNOWLEDGE
Building on the value of confidence, one quality that has allowed me to achieve long-term success as a trader is that

I know myself extremely well. As a trader, you are guaranteed to experience the full range of emotions. I am living proof of that. At the beginning, it is natural for emotions to sometimes get in the way. When you have a big day, it is natural to be happy—and when you lose, it is natural to be frustrated. As you grow and mature as a trader, the important thing is that you learn something about yourself each and every day.

You are always going to have winning days and losing days. In the long run, your level of success will be defined by how well you minimize the losers and maximize the winners. Not every trade will go in your favor. You do not even have to win on half your trades. The key is that when you are "on," you have big trades, big days, and big months. When you are not on top of your game, take it easy and make losses a non-event. Sounds easy, but the only way you can execute this simple plan is to know yourself and realize when you should push it or scale things back.

Knowing yourself well comes long after you have mastered the Xs and Os. I estimate the learning process takes at least two or three years depending on the person. Building "feel" is a matter of experience. Each losing day and each day of success serves as a way for you to evaluate yourself, to learn what worked and what did not. Some people never take the time to evaluate what they are doing and never reach their potential as a trader. So many traders are content after a good day to go out to happy hour right after the market closes. Likewise, a lot of guys just want to leave their desk as quickly as possible after a tough day. The only way you are going to learn about yourself is to take time after the close each day to evaluate each trade and how you managed the day overall. Did I trade setups I like? Did I define risk appropriately? I was feeling good today; did I make as much as I should have? I wasn't as prepared as I would have liked this morning, so was I patient and selective?

At the beginning of my career, I did not ask myself these difficult questions. In all honesty, there just did not seem to be a reason to question what I was doing. It was working. During that period I did not learn much about myself, except for the fact that I loved being successful and making money. I learned that Atlantic City was a fun place. I learned that the Greek Isles were beautiful, especially when you could afford to visit them aboard a fully-staffed yacht with your best friends. As a trader, though, I had yet to learn anything about myself. The big losses started to mount as the market went into a tailspin. School was now in session. They say you learn more from adversity than you do from success, and that was certainly the case for me over those couple of years. The process of learning about myself was long and painful. Bad habits cost me millions of dollars. In retrospect, that process of enduring pain and learning about myself set the stage for a decade of trading success.

> *The only way you are going to learn about yourself is to evaluate each and every trade; asking yourself the difficult questions.*

What does it mean to know yourself well? There are so many trading books and trading psychologists out there that spout pluralities about needing to know yourself, believe in yourself, and have supreme confidence. I agree with all those things, and after reading trading books, a light always seems to go on that says, "This is easy." The problem resurfaces the next time you sit down at your trading desk and experience a significant loss. That is the thing about confidence and knowing yourself—they have to be genuine qualities. Neither can be conditional, or else they are not genuine. As a young trader, I thought I was confident and thought I knew myself well, but both were fragile, temporary conditions. They were not real because the market conditions were not real. The slow grind that followed the tech boom allowed me to take my trading walkabout.

Risk Tolerance

The first step to knowing yourself as a trader is to understand how much risk you can tolerate on a regular basis. When things were good, I took big risks because things generally worked themselves out in my favor. When things were more difficult, I became significantly more risk-averse. Whereas earlier in my career, I always expected things to go in my favor, now a lot of my focus is on getting into trades where there is a clear stop.

Risk management does not receive enough attention from traders because it is not the most appealing aspect of the job. Everyone always asks me what my biggest days are. Few people want to hear about my big losing days because they are not "sexy". One thing I always say to traders I train is: "Good traders think about how much they can win on a trade. Great traders think about

The first step to knowing yourself as a trader is to understand how much risk you can tolerate on a regular basis.

how much they can lose on a trade." You must always have risk parameters for yourself. Boil it down to each trade and work your way up. I always set a firm stop for myself in any trade, no matter what. Although I have some long-term holdings as an investor, I do not aimlessly enter positions in my active trading account. Many traders will enter a position with their wide eyes set firmly on an ambitious price target. When the trade begins to go against them, doubt and regret creep in. What should have been a non-event becomes a damaging loss. You should always identify trades that possess a risk-to-reward ratio in your favor. For me, I only get into trades with a minimum of a 2-to-1 ratio, meaning my target is always twice as far away as my stop. That is not to say I arbitrarily set targets and stops to give myself that ratio. All chart setups I trade naturally lend themselves to having a favorable ratio. That is what trading is all about. With risk versus reward skewed in your favor, you will always make more on the winners than you lose on the duds.

Never enter a trade unless you know how much you stand to lose. If your risk parameters are undefined, a small loss can become a catastrophe. Once you have learned how to properly set stops and have disciplined yourself to adhere to them, then you should move onto the next step: setting a daily stop-loss point. Adjust loss limits based on recent performance and how lucrative the market has been. Tighten the controls when trading is more difficult to ensure you do not dig yourself a hole during slower periods. Always adhere to your lim-

> *Good traders think about how much they can win on a trade. Great traders think about how much they can lose.*

its, no matter how tempting it is to keep going. Trust me, I get the same urge, too. "I know I can make it back, I know I can turn it around today." More often than not, losses grow and you go home with an upset stomach. The next step is setting loss limits on a monthly basis. If you reach your loss limit for the month, it should tell you two things: your head is not right and the market is not good for trading. Even if it is just one of those things, you should be limiting how much you trade. As painful as it may be to shut it down for a month after you hit a loss limit, I promise it will be the best thing in the long run. As you approach a monthly loss limit, you should cut down your size and get back to the basics. Again, the key is not digging yourself a hole during a time when you probably did not stand to gain that much in the first place. During times when either you or the market are not "on," take it easy and live to fight another day.

Expectations

The next step is to be realistic with yourself in terms of expectations. After the dot-com bubble burst, I was forced to rein in my expectations because they were not realistic as the market changed. When you are taking fewer risks, inevitably you are going to have less potential reward. I had to make peace with that for the time being, and it was not easy. I had been making obscene profits during the tech boom, and I wanted so badly for it to go back to the way it had been. I had to learn to accept things that were out of my control and focus on what I could control. A lot of people who get into trading have a sense of entitlement. They think, "I am smart, I work hard, other people make money doing it, I deserve to make good money." Trading does not work like that. It is not about how much you deserve to make or even, sometimes, how many hours you put into it. In the end, it comes down to how self-directed you can be and how much you can learn about trading and about yourself. It took being realistic for me to right the ship and reach a new level. The market is cyclical. I accepted less when things were slow because I knew volatility would return. When market conditions are conducive to trading, I increase my expectations and put into practice the lessons learned during slower periods.

Just like managing risk, effectively managing expectations should begin on a micro level and grow from there. Depending on the market, stocks will trade in a different manner. Basically, there are two types of market conditions: a range-bound market and a breakout/breakdown oriented market. In a range-bound market, stocks tend to bounce around in a given range, bouncing off support and resistance levels, typically on lower volume. In a breakout/breakdown oriented market, stocks tend to only pause at support and resistance levels before making momentum moves higher or lower, generally on higher volume. You can make money in either type of market, but the ease and amount of money you make is likely to vary greatly. Typically in a range-bound market, stocks make shorter moves and each winning trade yields a relatively smaller profit. In a market full of breakouts and breakdowns, it is easier to capture big moves in stocks and each winning trade yields a relatively greater profit. To put it more simply, it is harder to make money in a low volume, rangy market.

First, you have to identify the type of market. If volume is low and stocks have a difficult time breaking through levels, you need to adjust your expectations. If stocks are regularly breaking out, you can expect more. This concept applies to each and every trade. Set targets based on the type of market, and tighten stops accordingly to maintain an advantageous risk-reward ratio. Be content to take smaller profits on trades if that is what the market dictates. Likewise, if conditions are good, make sure you take advantage.

Once you have adjusted your expectations on a trade-by-trade basis, it will grow naturally from there. Adjust your daily expectations based on how well the market is trading. If you have to take smaller profits on each trade, do not try to make up for it by putting on more trades. Actually, a range-bound market may dictate that you put on fewer trades and simply wait for more clear-cut setups to show their faces. Naturally, if you are taking smaller profits on each trade and putting on fewer trades, your days and months will be less profitable. It is not always easy being green. Do not panic if all of a sudden your income shrinks over a quarter or even over a six-month period; the next great opportunity is just around the corner. Learn your lessons when things are slow so that when they improve, you are more ready than ever to knock it out of the park.

Let Go

Another big step in knowing yourself well is being able to let things go. Being able to accept losses is one trait that definitely comes with time. You will not achieve any longevity in the business if you let each bad day take something out of you. Evaluate what went wrong, endeavor to learn from mistakes, and move on. If losses stick with you and affect performance the next day, it becomes a slippery slope.

A bad day becomes a bad week. A negative month becomes a negative year. Next thing you know, the enormity of the task becomes overwhelming and you hit rock bottom. I never became desperate financially, but the persistent losses definitely took a significant toll on my psyche and my mental health. Building myself back up was a long process. Now, being able to let things go is my greatest quality. I let things go because I have to. Just like building confidence, the ability to let things go has to be genuine. You can tell yourself all you want that you have forgotten about that recent loss. You can convince yourself that it will not affect your trading the next day, but that belief has to be genuine. You will know whether it is genuine when you go to put on your next big trade. If the setup is there, you should not hesitate to take the trade.

The ability to let things go comes from having balance in life. As much as you may think it helps to live, eat, and breathe trading, the high-stress nature of the business makes such a lifestyle unsustainable. You need to have outlets in order to relieve stress. When I was younger I was very active, played a lot of sports, and enjoyed an active social life with friends. Now, I am married, have children, and I look forward to going home to my family each day. Prioritize your life so that any gain or loss in trading is put into perspective. If you can leave the office each day to do something you love or enjoy, you will better be able to cope with the volatile nature of the job.

The ability to let things go comes from having balance in life.

Find Balance

You have established your risk tolerance and set realistic goals for yourself. You have conditioned yourself to let things go through a balanced lifestyle. Now how do you use these qualities to increase your trading returns? The area in which I really excel is getting the most out of the good days and good months in the market, and the reason I can do this is because I know myself. Each day in the markets is different, and if you take on any amount of risk in your trading, it is inevitable that you will have losing days. Also, each month is different. During the year, there are months with low volume and low volatility. There are months where the market is range-bound, when trading profits are more difficult. Especially in the summer months, volume is light as traders enjoy the weather and take vacations. Without major catalysts driving price movement, stocks can go into a relative lull at any time. When the action is slow, I do not press and am content to simply be green at the end of the month. The important thing is being aware of when the market is ripe for the picking, when stocks are bouncing around, when volume is high and good money can be made every day. Over the course of a few good months I generally make my year. During the slower months I maintain good habits, lighten up size, and lower expectations; but when conditions are good, I charge full steam ahead with full belief in my ability to read charts and analyze risk-to-reward scenarios.

I wait for two things to align before really pushing it during a trading day: the market and myself. Generally speaking, you can prevent losses or make a little when you have one factor present, but the days you are going to make your living are on the days when both conditions coincide. If I come into the office in the morning seeing charts clearly, and stocks are trading well that day, I will not leave my desk and I will look to get involved in a large number of stocks with large size. Those are the days when I put up six figures, when I start to push my account balance in the direction of my yearly goal. The reason I am able to separate myself from other traders on those days is because I know myself so well. I have a great feel for what my expectations should be on any given day and what my risk tolerance should be based on recent performance. I know whether I have the requisite focus required to trade effectively. I know if I am on, and when I am, I put the pedal to the metal.

To get to the next level as a trader, you have to be able to capitalize on the good days. You cannot let a past failure hold you back from pushing yourself outside of your comfort zone. Remind yourself that you know how to read charts and that you have put in the time to educate yourself. Push yourself. Maybe take on some additional calculated risks for the chance to get to that next level. Learn about yourself during these great days too. Take mental note of how good it feels to execute your game plan on a larger scale. Develop that muscle memory. The great days are what motivate me to do this job. During good periods in the market, I sit down at my desk with an excitement few people feel when they go to work each day. It is like an athlete getting ready for a big game. I look forward to the big moment because I am confident that I will execute.

Wait for two things to align before trading: the market and yourself.

PUTTING IT ALL TOGETHER

Trading is an unforgiving profession. Becoming a good trader takes a tremendous amount of experience and an ability to learn on the fly. In his book *Outliers*, Malcolm Gladwell estimates it takes 10,000 hours for an individual to become an expert in a given craft. For athletes, it takes years of taking jump shots and building confidence. For traders, it takes years filled with successes and failures to truly understand everything about the business. Unfortunately, most traders are forced to learn their most important lessons the hard way, and many never recover. Many people cannot handle the ups and downs of the business. Early on in my career, I knew I was wired for this job. Something about trading just gets my juices flowing in a positive way. Becoming a successful trader is like one enormous puzzle. Not everyone has the pieces, and even if they do, it takes a long time to put it together. If you can put it all together, it is an amazing feeling.

While I have always been involved in mentoring new traders and helping experienced ones get to another level, I have increased my focus on training over the last several years with T3 Live. With all of the technology resources and information available these days, traders in today's market no longer have to learn some of the lessons the hard way. While the strongest lessons are learned from personal experience, I hope that by sharing my experiences I can enlighten others about the pitfalls and keys to trading. If you take a disciplined approach to learning and trading, there is no reason why the learning curve cannot be shortened. The most important thing to understand is that the markets are always evolving. The reason I have been able to achieve consistent success and longevity in the business is because I have always been able to adapt. You must embrace change and strive to understand what it will take to succeed at every turn.

Life—and trading—will always bring ups and downs. There will always be obstacles to overcome. Adversity is inevitable. When you are faced with a problem or feel overwhelmed by the enormity of a task, you have three choices: you can run away from it, you can give up, or you can stand up to it and fight. The only way to conquer any challenge or correct personal inadequacies is to face up to them. Always evaluate yourself and take time to reflect. When you feel uncomfortable, be curious about your emotions and remain open to the task at hand. Do not ignore the problem or turn away from it. Attack it. When your confidence is shaken, use positive affirmations to remind yourself that you are a good trader. If you continue to probe and learn about yourself, you will not only be successful, but you will also be happy. If you are as passionate as I am about trading, the satisfaction of performing at a high level will transform your life.

> *The only way to conquer a challenge is to face up to it.*

• • •

10

Lessons from Scott

ONLY TEN YEARS AGO, THE WORLD WAS FULL OF OPTI-mism and hope as the curtain was raised on a new millennium. The technology sector was exploding due to the transformative power of the Internet, and investors were seeing incredible returns in their portfolios. Americans were spending like never before and the American Federal budget was running at a surplus. Fast forward to 2010, and the world is a very different place. The tech boom went bust. The 9/11 attacks led to a more cynical world and an unpopular war. The next bubble, this time in real estate, burst and triggered a domino effect in the world economy. The financial crisis of 2008 irreparably damaged the confidence of the American consumer and sent the market into a historic tailspin. The U.S. deficit has grown to dangerously high levels.

For too long, individuals and families have lived beyond their means. The corporate world has become plagued by scandal after scandal. The government swooped in to save the day and prevent a complete collapse of the financial system, and in the process, set a dangerous bailout precedent. It seems all sense of accountability has been lost. The public no longer knows who they can trust, and for good reason.

However, whenever you are faced with adversity, there is great opportunity to learn from mistakes. Educate yourself, do not follow the herd, and always be prudent. We have experienced the highs of the tech boom and the subsequent lows when the bubble burst. We felt the devastation of 9/11 in Manhattan. We anticipated the implosion of the real estate market and were prepared for the market collapse in 2008. We have seen just about every market imaginable, and we have made money in every single one. As the world rolls into a new decade, we want to share what we have learned with anyone who no longer wants to be at the mercy of the system.

Always have a plan, always be prepared, and always be accountable. In the end, you control your own destiny. All the resources you need to take control are out there. Hope is a powerful thing, and although we live in a cynical world, there is still much cause for optimism. The opportunity exists for us to emerge from this crisis stronger than we entered it, as individuals and as a country. It is time for the

Always have a plan, always be prepared, and always be accountable.

world to change. It is time for the individual to take control of their own future.

WHERE WE ARE NOW

The year 2008 was an eventful year for Americans and for traders. The buzz on the trading floor was deafening, the byproduct of unprecedented events. A perfect storm in the market had begun to violently rock the boat. Wall Street was a lightning rod of activity, and trading floors were especially lively. For the next six months, every trader showed up to work early and left late, craving the extraordinary action and volatility. It was like a natural disaster; the veterans who had been through similar times began shouting instructions to the wide-eyed throng of traders eager to take advantage of once-in-a-lifetime trading. The need to act quickly and decisively was paramount as doomsday fears sent stocks into a frenzy. Stocks bounced around wildly, making huge moves and delivering opportunities to those who were prepared. Eight years of calm followed the madness of the dot-com boom, but daytrading was back with a bang. After a prolonged bull market, another bubble had burst.

Bear Stearns went from one of the most respected banks in the world to a bankrupt embarrassment in a weekend. Still, it would have been impossible to predict how deep our financial system's problems went and how lucrative the next year would be for traders. The 12-month period beginning in early spring of 2008 with the sudden collapse of the 100-year-old firm was sadly one of the darkest in our country's history, as unemployment spiked to multi-decade high levels, capital for growth dried up, and the global economy headed into a tailspin. Gloom and doom prevailed as pundits forecasted a deep and long-lasting depression. Savings were going to evaporate, many said. Small businesses were going to be forced to shut their doors, others warned. The American Empire was set for an epic collapse on the scale of its Roman predecessors. Anyone and everyone was seeking advice on what to do with their money, no longer feeling it was safe anywhere but under the mattress. The second wave of rumors came, and then more failures. Fear of recession became fear of the economic apocalypse. Companies were not just reporting bad earnings; it was much worse than that. Staples of the American corporate landscape were going completely broke.

CONTROL YOUR OWN DESTINY

No one, including traders, likes to see despair. Economic problems affect us all. Many at our firm had friends and family lose jobs. Recessions write heartbreaking individual stories and present problems in the larger market for everyone. Still, as traders, it would be a lie to say we do not thrive amid the turmoil. Chaos brings opportunity. If you can slow things down and remain focused, you can take great advantage of the enormous volatility that accompanies economic pain.

Chaos brings opportunity. Traders can thrive amid turmoil by taking advantage of the enormous volatility that accompanies economic pain.

The great thing about being a trader is that you control your own destiny no matter what is going on around you. There are no excuses for your problems; all you can do is look into the mirror. During an economic downturn in this country, everyone looks to blame someone else. In this particular recession, an especially large amount of finger-pointing has been done—many feel the banks, with their derivative assets and astronomical bonuses, are at fault for all of our problems. Mortgage companies, trying to take advantage of uninformed borrowers with predatory lending, are culpable for the toxic assets plaguing balance sheets. The government, with its excessive spending, cronyism, and lack of oversight, is the root of the problem. All of these factors have led to an ever-growing gap between the haves and have-nots in this country and an ever-diminishing average quality of life.

The fact that these companies were able to get away with illegal activities, dressed up as contemporary, too-complicated-for-average-Joe-to-understand financial instruments that ultimately doomed the financial system is certainly an outrage. While all of these accessories are largely responsible for our deteriorating quality of life, it is naïve to reduce all problems to the inadequacies of other people. Americans put money in funds promising unreasonable returns on investment without educating themselves. Prospective buyers, blinded by their desire to call themselves "homeowners," took out mortgages with little money down and adjustable interest rates they had absolutely no chance of affording. The American electorate succumbed to the campaign for deregulation of Wall Street, voting for politicians who were in the pocket of big business. The one factor generally ignored is the man in the mirror.

Americans live beyond their means and save less than any nation in the world. The government's penchant for borrowing has cultivated a society where individuals focus on the short term. The subprime mortgage crisis and resultant global credit crisis were born out of financial irresponsibility across the board. Many individuals and families bought homes they could not pay for; others maxed out dozens of credit cards trying to outrun credit problems. The problem, in general, lies with dependence on credit, that we mortgage our futures for prosperity in the short-term. A sense of entitlement and ruthless greed defines many Americans and certainly our country's most successful and revered corporations. Individuals were willing to face the prospect of bankruptcy in the future in order to live like a king in the short term. By the time creditors came calling, the Ferraris and vacation homes were already several years old. As a people, we do not have a focus on the long-term and do not take accountability for our own fortunes. We are quick to blame others when things do not go our way.

You might find talk of long-term focus curious coming from an active trader, but not if you understand the principles of sound trading. Traders do not put their money and life in someone else's hands. Traders do not act irrationally when things begin to take a turn for the worse. Most of all, traders do not blame others for their problems, because they have taken control. Traders run their own businesses. When trading is good, traders put the pedal to the metal. When engines of volatility stall, we put it in park. When traders are making good money, they learn from what they are doing well. When we are losing, we must leave our frustration at the office and learn from each

Being a trader means that you control your own destiny no matter what is going on around you.

mistake. In trading, control lies entirely with the individual. The sense of independence in determining our lot is what makes the job rewarding.

THE TRADING MANTRA

To have success as an active trader, you can not just go through the motions. The only way to be profitable and meet your goals in the long run is to live your life by a mantra. Trading always mirrors life. If you lack preparation and discipline outside the office, it will always carry over into your trading. At the beginning of my career, I took a half-hearted approach and it was reflected in my profit and loss statement. The reason I got over the hump—and the reason I have continued to grow as a trader—is that I made a greater commitment to myself and my job. Everyone is different, and each individual has to make trading work for them. In my experience, however, it is impossible to sustain success without building certain habits and fully committing yourself to conquering the markets.

Trading is more than just a job, it is a lifestyle. The reason traders were able to profit during the 2008 economic crisis is that they understood the concept of risk management and prudency. While others were out buying homes and blindly throwing money into the markets, traders were being cautious and careful. The lessons you learn in becoming a consistently profitable trader teach you invaluable lessons outside of the job, too. Never risk more than you have, and never risk than you can stomach. Leverage and borrowing provide individuals and companies fuel for growth, but when they become excessive, you put yourself in a dangerous position. So when I say you must have a plan, it not only applies to the trading day. It applies to every day of your life. Also, without harmony outside of your trading or investing activities, you cannot perform to the best of your abilities.

You cannot approach trading as simply a job and expect to have consistent success. The emotional swings of the business, from day to day and year to year, make it too volatile for the faint of heart. If you do not have a firm plan in place, and balance in life to put success or failure in perspective, your career will crash and burn. Integrate trading into a larger vision you have for yourself, and trade according to an overarching set of values that encompass your life. Do not chase bubbles, do not chase stocks. When everyone else is getting overly exuberant and greedy, take a step back and evaluate the situation in a reasonable way. Most of the time, when excitement reaches climactic levels, it signals the coming of a collapse. That is what happened during the tech boom, and that is what happened in 2008. If you are prudent and planned, not only do you avert potential disaster to yourself personally, you can make money on the other side of the trade.

Something that has always irked me is that a lot of people have a negative perception of active trading, or "daytrading." In the last few years, I hope people have begun to understand the merits of actively managing assets, rather than buying and hoping the powers-that-be conduct themselves in a responsible manner. Whether you are trading professionally or actively managing a personal portfolio, taking personal responsibility for your own finances is a powerful feeling.

Building a Routine

The first step in creating success for yourself, especially as a trader, is building a routine that works for you. While everyone has a different way of doing things, there are certain characteristics of your routine and habits that should always be present. My personal mantra revolves around the principles of discipline and preparation. At the core of any routine should be a strong work ethic. Some individuals are predisposed to be good traders, but most of us require a great deal of work and self-evaluation. Building good habits takes time, and along the way you will learn what works and what does not.

I am a creature of habit; every one of my days is more or less the same. The disciplined nature of my routine allows me to quickly identify what is off if I am not making money. When you have structure and everything is the same, it becomes easy to diagnose and correct problems. Each morning, I wake up before 6:00 a.m. to give myself time to get prepared. I take the ferry into our lower Manhattan trading floor from my home in Jersey City, and on the ride I begin my research for the day by reading the *Wall Street Journal* and *Investor's Business Daily*. Once I get to my desk at 7:00 a.m., I already have a strong feel for the major news stories of the day and what stocks are going to be in play. I also consult Briefing. com and a few other media outlets to gather other pieces of information that could impact the markets.

After I have done my research, I begin to build my price point sheet. If you are a follower of T3 Live, you are probably familiar with my Morning Gameplan. My gameplan is a thorough and detailed rundown of my entire basket of stocks.

Building a watch list is an extremely important and under-valued aspect of being a consistently profitable trader. You have to have a group of stocks that you know well. In most cases, not every one of your stocks is going to be in play every single day, so you have to have different stocks in different sectors to which you can turn. For me, I generally have 30 to 40 stocks that I am intimately familiar with. Trading these stocks pays my bills and will pay for my son's college tuition.

On the price point sheet, I go through charts for every single one of the stocks on my watch list, and take note of important levels. I write down the trigger buy and sell prices as well as primary and secondary price targets. I make notes of the important things to consider about each stock, and give an overall rundown of the broader market to put everything in context. I identify stocks that are ripe for a reversal trade, one of my favorite trade setups that presents terrific risk-reward parameters.

On the surface, I build the Morning Gameplan to help T3 Live subscribers be prepared for the trading day and get in the head of a professional trader. But, to be honest, I would still build the price point sheet each morning even if there were no T3 Live. Building that watch list and going through each and every one of my stocks allows me to be fully prepared for almost every opportunity that presents itself. At 8:45 a.m., I shoot my Morning Call video on T3 Live, where I share my research and go over the price point sheet for that day. For me, going through stocks in the video continues to reinforce what stocks I should be looking at that day.

The preparation is the hard part. If you put in the work to prepare, proper execution will naturally follow. It is just like being an athlete. You gain skills and confidence from practice and preparation, so that when the big moments arise you are equipped for success. Once you have established a routine, it becomes second nature. Some people are astonished as to how much I do before the trading day. I do my own research, make my own detailed watch list, do my own commentary on the T3 Live blog, and send my notes out to the media, all before 8:00 a.m. But to me, it all just comes naturally now because I have made that routine a habit.

Finding Balance

The most important thing in my mind is preparation, but you also have to learn to navigate the trading day effectively. Everyone has their own attention span, so it is important to listen to your own body to know when you should and should not trade. I thrive on being disciplined and following a game plan, so when I start to deviate from my plan is when I take a step back. During unusually volatile days and periods in the market, I will stay at my desk all day every day. For the majority of trading days, however, I emphasize the need to have balance.

Obviously, being active is a big part of what now defines my life and even my career. Around lunchtime, you can almost always find me at the gym swimming, biking, or running. I make most of my money during the first and last hours of trading. Although I do sometimes miss trades during the middle of the day, my overall results are improved as a result of my midday routine. I encourage traders to be physically active as a way to reduce stress and reenergize your body, but there are also other ways to go about the trading day. The important thing is to be efficient. Make the bulk of your profits during the periods of the day when you generally excel. Do not give money back because you are tired or bored. Do not get hurt in a trade when volume is light and the market is less predictable. Whether it be exercise, simply taking a walk, or going out to lunch, do what it takes for you to maintain focus and be efficient.

The same concept applies to what you do after the trading day and on the weekend. Traders who maintain a high stress level always have short careers. Trading is a stressful job, and the bad days always hurt, no matter how good or experienced you are. To achieve longevity as a trader, you have to find ways to relieve stress and enjoy your life. Being a successful trader is not just about excelling at your trading desk, it is about constructing a lifestyle that allows you to be happy, healthy, and focused. In my experience, anytime there is disharmony in another part of your life, it carries over into your trading. My ability to let a bad trade go disappears. My tendency to dwell on a bad trade, bad day, or bad week increases. When building a vision and plan for your trading career, do not simply focus on the trades. Be realistic with yourself, and place an emphasis on health and happiness. I have always been a social animal, someone who likes to party and have a good time. That part of my personality allowed me to excel as a party planner and an emcee at weddings and bar mitzvahs. After becoming a trader, I continued to use my social life as an outlet to relieve stress and enjoy my life. If you have a good day, do not hesitate to celebrate with other traders or friends. If you have a good month, take a vacation and reward yourself. If you have a bad morning, do not be afraid to take the rest of the day off to recharge your batteries and relieve stress.

Thinking Ahead

In addition to preparing for each day, I try to identify more long-term trends in the market and different sectors. Some people like to say they use technical analysis and fundamental analysis together when investing, but that is often difficult and in the end, one of the principles takes precedence over the other. I like to think that I use a combination of technical analysis and common sense. First and foremost, I use charts as an unbiased indicator of future prices, but if economic factors or broad market sentiment contradict what I see in a chart, I am cautious. Likewise, if a chart pattern aligns with common sense, I will have more conviction and be more aggressive.

Back in 2008 during one of my CNBC appearances, I highlighted gold as the trade to watch for the next 12 months. When I made the call, I remember being mocked by some other pundits who saw my predictions as outlandish. The chart was forming a bullish head and shoulders pattern, and several other factors were telling me that gold was poised to explode above the 1000 per ounce price level. The financial crisis triggered a flight to safety for investors as they saw their equity holdings greatly decrease in value. When volatility and fear increase to extreme levels, investors seek to move their money into something they can see and touch. Gold became that safe haven. The United States government began printing money to bail out failing banks and automotive companies, bringing fears of future hyperinflation. Everything pointed to an explosive and measured move in gold in 2009, and that is exactly what we got. CNBC began to regularly call me back in to discuss how I was maneuvering the trade. At a time when many people were too fearful to invest their money, I guided our T3 Live community and T3 traders through the gold trade. The gold trade was a powerful example of my trading philosophy in action.

Most people are doomed for failure in trading before they even buy or sell their first stock. The stock market is a cruel place. The unprepared are wiped clean before they know what happened. People are by nature greedy. Someone hears a tip about a hot up-and-coming stock that they have to own and feel obligated to "invest." Many risk money they can not afford to lose, hoping they have found the company reinventing the wheel. Everyone looks for the next get-rich-quick scheme, hoping to leverage a lifetime of modest earnings into a lavish fortune. These people do not have a plan for success. They jump into the action without first doing their homework. They let losers run until they wipe out their accounts, and allow winners to turn into losers. Without preparing psychologically for trading or investing, they are doomed for failure no matter what they buy.

What separates these people from successful investors is that they do not have a plan. To have success in any endeavor, you must have a plan. First, you must define your goals and expectations. Without knowing what you want and expect to reasonably get out of trading and investing, it is impossible to develop a plan. The next step is actually doing your homework to develop a plan. Many people search the Internet looking for the latest hot system for trading. If you are constantly searching for easy, no-effort profits, you are going to be disappointed. There are many technical strategies and indicators out there, many of which can be completely contradictory. You are best-served to find a simple strategy that fits your personality and stick with it. Find a community of like-minded investors that can help you master the emotional roller coaster of trading. Take advantage of access to professionals as much as possible. Speaking with pros will not get you all the answers, but it will help you understand what it takes from a psychological standpoint.

The process of learning about yourself as a trader takes time. While taking time to educate yourself is important, thinking about trading is not anywhere close to the same thing as actually doing it. Trading is baptism by fire. Practicing on a simulator serves its purpose. You can learn the keys, you can practice execution, and you can simulate strategies to a certain degree, but the real learning starts when you first set foot in those trenches. During your first months as a trader, your goal should be to soak up as much information as possible and start to build a routine that will set the stage for success in the future. Once your routine is established, it is important to continue to push yourself to be more efficient and dynamic.

●●●

11

Lessons from Evan

A BUSINESS PLAN

PEOPLE OFTEN DO NOT UNDERSTAND WHAT I MEAN WHEN I say you need to create a business plan for yourself as a trader. They think, "I am a trader, not a small business owner." Trading is different from any other job, but in essence, you are still running your own small business. No matter what type of trader you are or what your goals are in the market, it is important to put those things in writing so you have a frame of reference for maintaining discipline. Writing a comprehensive business plan is the first step in building accountability. The process of learning what you are good at takes time and effort. At the beginning of your trading career, your focus should be on identifying personal strengths as a trader rather than dwelling on profit and loss numbers. It will be impossible to ever see consistently positive results if you do not plan for success.

In building your business plan, the first question you must ask yourself is: what are my values? Defining your values will help you begin to build expectations and craft your trading style. What do you seek to gain from a career as a trader on a financial, personal, or spiritual level? Many people cannot answer this question when they start trading. Do you value a steady paycheck each month to support a family, or are you looking to supplement your income by trading selectively on the side? Are you entering the business to give yourself greater control or freedom? Defining your goals as a trader or investor will help you stay on the right track and make the right decisions. What are you willing to commit to your business in terms of capital, time, and energy?

Many traders enter the business because, from afar, it seems like an attractive lifestyle with significant earning potential. You make it into the office at 9:30 a.m. and can leave at 4:00 p.m. when the market closes. Are you only willing to do the bare minimum or are you willing to fully invest in trading? You need to match what you are willing to put into it with your expectations. It is not reasonable to think you can make a living as a trader without a massive level of commitment of time, energy, and emotion. How will you evaluate yourself? What will you do if your business is not successful? Most people do not come up with a plan for evaluating themselves. When they are faced with adversity, they panic because they did not plan for failure. Failure is a temporary condition, and every trader faces obstacles before becoming successful. You must be prepared for every scenario that may come your way. Before making your first trade, build a business plan and answer these important questions.

FINDING STRENGTHS

A large part of being successful is knowing what you do well. Many people get caught up trying to be something they are not, and get caught up making trades into something they are not. To have a successful career in any field, you really just need to do one thing very well. Shaq does not try to shoot three-pointers and Steve Nash does not try to enter the slam dunk contest. I know what I do well, and what I do not do so well. I do not excel at short-term scalping strategies. I am at my best when I am being patient and waiting for my perfect trade.

An individual should always try to align strengths and goals when choosing a career. For example, a student who excels in reading and writing should not pursue a goal of becoming a rocket scientist, and a talented math student should not aim to become a journalist. The same concept applies to traders. Some may be drawn to a specific style of trading because of the results they see other traders achieving with that style, but it may not be the best strategy for them. Some could be enticed by the consistent profits a scalp trader enjoys, but not have the requisite focus and discipline to execute such a strategy. In contrast, another individual could be drawn to swing trading because of the potential for large profits on each trade, but not possess the necessary degree of patience. You must strive to identify what you do well as a trader and build a style that maximizes your talents, rather than setting a goal and trying to force a square peg into a round hole. The only way to work towards identifying the style that is best for you is to build a business framework.

What is going to separate you from the pack? The reality is that most people do not make money trading. The majority of market participants are primitive. They cannot separate emotions from the rational mind, and do not have a consistent plan of action. To consistently make money, you have to avoid the temptation to follow the herd. You have to do something that separates you.

A large part of being successful is knowing what you do well.

SIMPLE DOES NOT MEAN EASY

Trading is not easy. Trading is simple. In this case, the words "easy" and "simple" are not synonyms. The distinction is very important. Trading is simple, as in straightforward, uncomplicated, and unadorned. It is not easy, as in undemanding, effortless, and trouble-free. The reason people often run into problems in trading is because they expect the opposite— they expect the process to be complicated, but results to come easily. Traders think if they use the hottest and most complex new indicator, they are smarter than everyone else, and thus assured of coming out on top. The reason it is not easy is because people make it more difficult than it has to be. I am not a genius. I do not think my ideas are revolutionary. In my opinion, I am the Average Joe trader. The reason I have been able to have consistent success is that I have made trading work for me. I make things easy for myself.

A lot of people make trading out to be some sort of ultra-sophisticated practice. Investors see technical analysis as some sort of voodoo, charts full of squiggles and lines too advanced to bother with. People are afraid of technical analysis and skeptical of active trading. My question is, why? What people do not realize is that trading is only as complicated as you make it. You do not have to use a dozen different indicators or even trade multiple stocks each day. An individual has limitations as to how much they can reasonably expect to comprehend and manage at one time. Embrace that fact. One trade a day, even one trade a week, can make you a lot of money.

Furthermore, you do not have to be a genius to succeed as a trader. Being "smart" can even become an obstacle for some people. The smarter you think you are, the more you will get in your own way. There are hundreds of chart studies and trading strategies out there. Each has its own merits, and most of them may work to a certain degree if executed correctly. The key part of that sentence is, "if executed correctly." Many strategies look strong in backtesting models, but future results are unpredictable, because past results are simply fit to a curve. Also, what can one person execute with confidence on a consistent basis? You must be able to build yourself a game plan that you can expect to replicate. Do not bite off more than you can chew. In addition, many indicators are directly contradictory. If you pay attention to every new tool, strategy, or indicator, you will run yourself in circles and drive yourself crazy in the process.

In the end, stocks only do three things: move up, down, or sideways. It is as simple as that. When people come to me overwhelmed about their trading, I remind them of this simple fact—up, down, and sideways. If you can, in your mind, begin to simplify trading in that way, it is a good start in making life easy for yourself. The only focus a good technical trader has is on price and price itself. While it is important to understand the macroeconomic climate and news on stocks you are trading, the most objective indication of future price movement will always be past price movement. Most people just do not understand the nature of technical analysis and why it works.

> *In the end, stocks only do three things: move up, down, or sideways.*

WHY TECHNICAL ANALYSIS WORKS

Let's break it down in very simple terms. Technical analysis is the study of prices, which are dictated by buying and selling. Charts give us the opportunity to analyze and track price in an efficient manner. Buying and selling are the result of human emotions; the reactions of individuals and institutional traders to movement and news.

So, if prices represent human emotions, and technical analysis is the study of prices, then, in essence, technical analysis is the study of human emotion. Candlesticks, pivot points, retracements, and bases are reflections of the emotions of the people trading the stock. The people who understand the nature of the game and become the masters of their emotions are the ones who consistently come out ahead. Do not get caught up in the same mode of reactionary trading as others.

Just like in a game of poker, it is less about playing the cards than it is about understanding the tendencies of the other players at the table. It does not matter if you have if you are holding a hand of 2-7 or pocket aces. As a trader, it does not matter if you are trading AIG or AAPL. The chart gives you a window into what other market participants are thinking and doing. You just need to know how to read the chart, and that is what technical analysis is all about. Through candlestick analysis, you can draw invaluable clues about what other traders are doing. You can tell when shorts are getting squeezed or when institutions begin to accumulate large positions. You can tell when a strong stock needs to take a rest or retrace some of its move.

To be honest, you can look at a chart and see just about anything you want if you let biases get in the way. People often use charts to confirm a pre-existing bias, or to justify a stubborn point of view. If someone thinks the President is lousy and the economy is going down the tube, they will search for a bearish pattern to align with their preconceived notion. Trading with a bias will always get you in trouble, because you are not letting the price action dictate your trades. Everyone wants to have an opinion, but you have to fight the urge to make trading subjective. A phrase I often use to simplify this concept for traders is, "follow the path of least resistance." The path of least resistance is the direction or course a stock will most likely take based on its chart. If there are significant obstacles to a stock moving in one direction, the overwhelming majority of the time, it will go the other way. If you can identify the charts with the fewest number of roadblocks, you will be on your way to becoming a highly successful trader. Charts tell stories.

Charts tell you where a stock wants to go. Let the price action do all the talking.

VISUALIZING TRADING SUCCESS

Psychologists often preach visualization as a powerful ingredient for success. Athletes are taught to visualize the ideal play. A baseball player visualizes a balanced swing resulting in a line drive. A basketball player visualizes taking a pass and making the shot in rhythm using proper form. With a picture in his mind of what the perfect play looks like, the player executes almost flawlessly when the big moment comes. The combination of visualization and building muscle memory will lead to a desired result on a consistent basis for an athlete. In trading, all of the same concepts apply. You should visualize your perfect trade before it happens and take mental note of how you execute good trades.

For me, there was a time when I was not a very planned trader. Much like the rest of the T3 team, I began my career during the tech boom and the environment did not necessitate a whole lot of planning. I bought a stock, it went up, I sold, waited for the dip, and bought again. I did not come into the office early to build a game plan. I did not stay long after the close to analyze my trades. Post tech boom, everyone had to change and I found the transition especially difficult. While some others were able to adapt, initially I was one of the people shaken out. My bad habits had become so ingrained they were difficult to break. I did not know how to make money. I did not know what my perfect trade looked like.

Today, I am meticulous in my preparation because that is what it takes for me to be successful. Visualization is a big part of what I do. I know what my perfect trade looks like and I know how to execute. If I ask you, "What is your strategy? What does your perfect setup look like?" you should be able to very clearly explain it to me. There was a point in my career when someone asked me those same questions and I did not have a good answer. Once I finally had an answer, I turned the corner as a trader.

Every morning, I arrive at the office well before the open to go over my watch list of stocks. Twice a week, I hold morning meetings with T3 traders where I go over charts I am following closely. Each day, I record my Trade for Thought video for T3 Live, in which I give a detailed breakdown of my favorite swing trade at that moment, which includes detailed entry signals and measured targets. First, when evaluating a stock, you must understand how it trades relative to the market. If you are in a bear market and stocks trade lower across the board, you are not going to be looking for longs. You are going to be looking for the especially weak stocks, the ones that are unable to bounce on days when the market comes up for air. Likewise, in a raging bull market, you are not going to be looking for long-term short setups.

The problem is that the majority of markets are not so clear cut. The reason active trading trumps buy-and-hold investing is because most market environments are more ambiguous. Rarely is it as simple as "things are going up across the board," or "every stock is getting slammed." Those types of markets do exist, and I am the first one to recognize them and be more aggressive initiating longer term positions. Examples of those markets include the tech boom as well as the market meltdown of 2008. Still, if you want to have consistent cash-flow from trading activities, you have to learn how to identify trades within a series of different market environments, especially more range-bound markets. So, while I do analyze broad market sentiment, the majority of my trade ideas come from analyzing charts to identify the strongest and weakest stocks. It all comes back to the charts. I look for technical patterns that indicate where a stock is most likely to go. I wait patiently for the trade to come to me, and give my idea the chance to play out with measured stops and targets.

THE VALUE OF PATIENCE

An athlete I greatly admire is Barry Bonds. Steroids issue aside, he is one of the greatest baseball players of all time. I admire how he plays not because of his tremendous power or once-dynamic speed. Bonds is a great hitter and a winner because he does not swing at every pitch that thrown his way. Even if a pitch is a strike, he may not even consider swinging—because it is the not the pitch he wants, not the one he knows he can hit for a home run. Bonds was a great player because of his eye at the plate, his patience in waiting for exactly the right pitch for him to deliver in the outfield or over the fence. All it took was one pitch a game and he could make the key difference in the overall outcome. If he needed to take a walk and come back up to bat again, he had no problem doing that. Barry Bonds led the league in on-base percentage because he was prepared to wait for his pitch.

The value of patience in baseball runs parallel to the value of patience in trading. Many traders perform poorly because they chase trades. The market dictates how aggressive you should be in your trading. Market volatility varies during the week and during the year, and changes given the economic environment. Understanding when to be aggressive and when to take a walk can be the difference between treading water and thriving as a trader. Many give profits back trying to trade on a Friday in the summer, when trading is slowest. Many put themselves in debt trying to capture large follow-through moves in a market bound in a tight range. Context is very important in trading, because without volume and volatility, you will at best churn in place. Before anything else, you must understand what inning you are in and what the score is. Sure, women dig the long ball and rich traders, but those always chasing home runs and big money trades in all situations strike out more often than not. When I wait for exactly the right setups, for all the factors to align before entering a trade, while they were not always home runs, my batting average has proven outstanding.

While I would never equate trading to gambling, there is another analogy I like to use to explain my approach to active trading. Each trade is like a hand of blackjack. In blackjack, the house almost always wins in the long run because you are forced to play every hand you are dealt. Even if you get an unfavorable deal, you are still required to keep your skin in the game and likely lose the bet. As a trader, you are presented with similar decisions as you are at the blackjack table. The major difference is, however, that as a trader, you do not have to play every hand. You can play only the hands that have a high likelihood of success. If you get a bad deal, you can walk away from the table without putting money in the pot. If you receive a promising set of cards, you can evaluate the landscape and place a bet. Under that scenario, you—not the house—win in the long run. If blackjack were like trading, trips to Atlantic City and Vegas would be even more fun. As traders, we are afforded the luxury of being able to choose what hands to play, and if you are patient and selective you will come out on top in the end.

THE VALUE OF EDUCATION

The value of education is the most overlooked aspect of trading, both for new and experienced traders. The need for ongoing education is paramount if you want to have long-term success. Traders are by nature very confident people, sometimes to a fault. When a young trader enters the business, they are chomping at the bit to get started. While they are eager to learn, they are more eager to start trading live and making money. As an experienced trader and mentor, it is my job to slow these individuals down. On the other hand, experienced traders think that they never need to get back in the classroom, so to speak. They feel entitled to success because they have been in the business for years. They think they are too good for seminars and do not need to read books because they have learned it all before. It is my job to remind these individuals that there is always room for improvement.

Wait for exactly the right setups, for all the factors to align before entering a trade.

The reason I stress the importance of education for traders is because I am a trader, and I have been there. At the beginning of my career, I scoffed at the idea of reading books and going through training courses because I was finding success at that time. "If it ain't broke, don't fix it," I thought. What I did not understand is that success, like failure, is a temporary condition. Success is not sustainable if not built on a firm foundation of knowledge and understanding.

When the tech boom went bust, I was caught with my pants down. For more than a year, I went to my desk each morning without a plan for making money, without the tools I needed to find success. I lost a lot of money and all of my confidence. Only after a prolonged period of hardship did I make the commitment to educating myself, and transforming my trading and my life. I put in the time and made the commitment to myself to get educated. The reason I have been able to adapt to changing markets since the tech boom is that I have not stopped learning. I am always reading a book about trading or blogs by other traders. Finding books I have not read is now my greatest challenge. I am always seeking out other traders to hear their take on the market. I embrace the assumption that there is always someone out there who is smarter than me and a better trader than me.

Success, like failure, is a temporary condition.

When I go through rough patches in my trading, I do not press or try to stubbornly push through it like some other traders. I take a step back and learn something new that could potentially make me better. When I am learning new things, I do not always incorporate them into my own trading. I know what I am good at. Still, you can gain a greater understanding of the market if you know what other people out there are doing. Other traders are my competition for the limited profits out there in the market, and if I am not tuned in to what they are doing, I will be the prey. I always strive to be the aggressor, the predator, the one who gets the prime cut while everyone else is fighting it out for the scraps.

I have become an educator because I love helping other traders reach their potential. While I am a swing trader, I have been effective in helping all types of traders understand what is holding them back. To be perfectly honest, I also value my role as an educator for selfish reasons. Teaching others makes me a better trader. When I am teaching others, I become even more aware of what I am doing and hold myself to an even higher standard. Teaching serves to reinforce the principles that drive my success. I recommend all traders try to become teachers in some capacity. Even if you are new and inexperienced, bounce your ideas off other traders. The more you talk about the technique and psychology of trading, the more it will become ingrained in your mind.

No matter what level of experience or type of trader you are, you will always benefit from learning something new. If you are relatively new to active trading, I strongly encourage you to educate yourself before making your next move in the market. Get help building your business plan. The money you will spend becoming educated will pale in comparison to the money you will save yourself in the markets. Attend a seminar with real professional traders to understand what separates them from amateurs. Join a community that will help you identify opportunities and give you a standard for evaluating performance. Every day, you should read something that expands your understanding of the market or enhances your self-awareness. Every week, you should watch a webinar or attend a trader meeting and listen to what other traders are saying. Every month, at least, you should read a new trading book. Remember, success is temporary and there are always others out there working harder than you. In the long run, the only way you will come out ahead is if you continue to educate yourself every day.

T3 TIP ....

Check out T3Live's Education Programs on T3Live.com.

• • •

12

Lessons from Nadav

THE POWER OF A POSITIVE MINDSET

WHILE MY TECHNICAL EXPERTISE AND FAST EXECU-
tion have certainly had a large role to play in my
success, they are useless to a trader without the
right mindset. Yes, I put in countless hours at the beginning of my career learning the nuances of the markets. It
took months for me to master the intricacies of the scalp
trading method. Yes, I continue to study different trading
techniques as a part of my ongoing education, something
that is vital in an ever-changing market. Education is vitally
important for one to become long-run profitable as a trader.
However, the technical knowledge I have gained does not
dictate my rate of success. The most important ingredient in
my success has been my positive attitude.

Most traders discount the need for constant psychological evaluation. No, I do not think you need to go see a trading therapist every week, but yes, I do think you need to evaluate yourself in that regard every day. When they hit a rough patch, the majority of traders think they are doing something wrong. They are right, but not in the sense that their strategy is flawed or they need to adjust their technique. These traders are letting small miscalculations become major problems. Bad trades, bad weeks, and bad months snowball if you let them. A period of prolonged losses drives most people out of the business.

Embracing Loss

Failures and losses are an inevitable part of life. On both a professional and personal level, going through a loss is difficult, even if you are expecting it. As a trader, losses make you uncomfortable and fill you with regret. "Why did I do that? I just gave away my whole month!" There is no way to train your mind to completely erase all of these types of thoughts because it is our nature, and part of what makes us human. What you can do, and what I have always been able to do, is frame things in a certain mindset—a positive mindset. There are a thousand books out there about trading education and psychology and they all say the same thing. Be rational, not emotional. Do not be emotional at all when you trade. Separate your thoughts and your emotions. I agree with those ideas wholeheartedly. Being emotionless would be ideal for a trader. The problem is that we are people, not robots. Unless something is completely out of whack with your physiology, it is impossible to be emotionless.

The key is not letting your emotions paralyze you, but rather being aware and using them as motivation to improve yourself. Embrace the fact that there will be losses and there will be failures. If you go through life thinking that things will always be peachy and you will never have to deal with loss, when it does come, you will not be equipped to handle it, and it will consume you.

This directly applies to trading. Many people enter the business thinking they will definitely be taking home a big fat paycheck after the first month. They heard about professional traders who made $100,000 in one day and wonder why they can not do it too. What they do not realize is that there is a learning curve. Success can come, but not before lessons are learned, and usually the hard way. These people are caught off guard by failures, unequipped to deal with them. The rug will be pulled on everyone, and not only when you are a new trader. Traders who have been in the business for years will experience crushing losses, but the ones who have survived since the tech boom are those who have been able to roll with the punches.

T3 TIP ···
You must have a realistic framework for success. In my experience, it takes 6 to 12 months for a trader to become profitable.

Embracing loss does not mean that you are okay with it. If you are competitive and want to make money, losses should never sit well with you. Embracing loss means that you understand its inevitability and are prepared for everything that comes with it. The fiercest competitors and the best traders are often those who are most bothered by losses, the ones who want to avoid that feeling as much as possible. The ones who fail are those who fold when they hit those bumps in the road, the ones who allow their failures to dictate their mindset going forward. While good traders definitely hate losing, they do not dwell on it.

The important thing to understand about any loss is that life will go on no matter what. As a trader and a person, you must frame each hardship with this question: How can I become stronger? No matter how disheartening, every loss or failure is an opportunity to improve. Life goes on, how can I learn from this? How will I proceed? There are two choices. One, you can dwell on the negatives of the situation, repeating to yourself what you did wrong and how worthless or unlucky you are. Two, you can instead frame it as what you can learn from the situation. Focusing on negatives gets you nowhere. Feeling sorry for yourself gets you nowhere. If you limp out of the carnage with your ego and your confidence battered, it is only a matter of time before things get worse. You cannot eliminate all inklings of regret and frustration, but you have the power to alter the way you proceed onward from seemingly negative events.

Choosing Positivity

Having a positive mindset will help you be more happy and successful in life before it ever affects your trading. I believe that in a lot of ways I was predisposed to being a good trader, but I have definitely learned the value of a positive mindset throughout my life. I stayed positive when I went to a different school than all my friends. Coming to America as a teenager, I had to deal with uncertainty alone. When I squandered my tuition money, I had to climb my way out of the doldrums. Talk about adversity and loss. The trading psychology book would have told me "be rational, not emotional." I had just lost thousands of dollars my parents had given me to pay for college in a far-off country. Needless to say, I felt a range of emotions. I felt guilt, despair, regret, loneliness—the whole gamut of negative human emotions.

Feeling emotion is natural and it triggers a response. For me, these emotions were healthy because they reminded me I could not afford to take such risks. Human beings, over the course of our evolution, have learned from mistakes and figured things out. I had to tap into my survival instincts from that point on, and the result was that I came out the other side a stronger person. There were days I did pity myself, when the loneliness and regret were almost more than I could handle. In the end though, through much introspection, I said to myself, "Life goes on, how I proceed from here is my choice." I did not let my failure consume me, but I set out to get back on my feet little by little. I could not make back all the money I lost in one day or one month; I would have to reconstruct myself and my life from the ground up.

From that point on, any setback in my life seemed somewhat mild. I think in a lot of ways, my style of trading was the result of the struggles I went through to get back on my feet. Without any money left, trading was not an option. My life turned into a grind. Seemingly every hour of the day I was in class, studying, or at work. When I first started trading, I tried to hit a home run and struck out. The next opportunity I got to trade, I did not take such a reckless approach.

TRUE CALLING

The reason I am a great trainer is because I bring more to the table than just technical knowledge and expertise. The difference between the education we provide at T3 Live and the education you receive from other places is that we are real traders who are in the trenches every day. Whether it be training our hedge fund traders or individuals who come to our seminars, we do not sugarcoat things. I have experienced the ups and downs and the emotional swings. I know what it is like to throw everything away and what it is like to make the breakthrough.

When I was training traders, I would always make an effort to make everything as colorful as possible. If you think back to middle school or high school, what teachers do you remember the most? You remember the ones who made the material come to life, and not only do you remember the teacher, but you remember the information. That is the approach I take when teaching new traders. The lively metaphors are what make people remember what it means when there is BIG size on the bid. In the same way, I make sure young traders understand the psychological challenges they will face. A lot of traders choose to ignore their bad days. They pretend like they never happened. To me, that is cheating everyone else. I have learned so much from my darkest days, it would be selfish not to impart those lessons on a new generation of traders.

Once you have gained a tremendous amount of experience in the markets or become a professional, everyone has generally the same level of knowledge. Each trader knows his or her perfect setup and how their favorite stocks move. The difference between the good and great trader lies in their mastery of the psychological aspect.

Strength and Weakness

A simple way to look at your development as a trader is to list your strengths and your weaknesses. When you start trading, the list is very one-sided. You can get all the education you want, but until you actually go live on the trading floor, you have not really learned anything. The concepts of active trading are simple. The hard part is executing them. The only way to grow as a trader is to continue to learn on the fly. You have to be able to understand what is happening, what is holding you back, and what mistakes you are making. It is okay to make mistakes as long as you do not repeat the same ones.

Each time you make a mistake or experience a loss, evaluate why that loss occurred. Were you selective enough? Was your entry sloppy? Were you greedy with your price target? If you approach each trade with a positive mindset, you can turn each result, positive or negative, into a learning experience. Still, you always learn more from mistakes than successes. Each time you lose, focus on identifying the reason and switching it over to the other column. Slowly, that list will start to become more balanced and even unbalanced in the other direction. Any trader will tell you, no matter how long they have been in the business, the learning process is ongoing. There will always be things you can do better. Bad habits will present themselves. The key is taking every opportunity to learn from your mistakes.

For a scalp trader, psychology is an especially large part of what you do. A momentum trader makes a lot of trades throughout the day in quick succession, so it is important to be on your game on a consistent basis. Scalping is intense and if you are off your game mentally, things can spiral out of control quickly. The only way to right a sinking ship is to slow down and start over.

> *It is okay to make mistakes—as long as you do not repeat the same ones.*

BUILDING A GOOD TRADER

When trying to explain the development of a good trader, I like to use the metaphor of building a house. The first step in building a house is setting the foundation. The foundation in trading is getting a complete education. You have to put in the time and effort to learn. In trading, there are so many factors you need to be aware of. You must understand how the market works and how stocks move. You must gain a detailed knowledge of technical analysis and be able to interpret several different indicators simultaneously. When building a house, many people forget about the importance of laying a good foundation because it is not sexy. There is no glamour in pouring the concrete, in putting in the classroom hours, but nonetheless, it is crucial to building the house. If you build a solid foundation, it will be there forever. Many years down the line, you may have to fill in a small crack, but a strong foundation never crumbles.

The next step is building the frame. After putting in the hours to learn about the markets and different styles of trading, you must settle on a style that fits your personality.

Many traders get caught up in trying to be something they are not. In my case, I was initially drawn to trading because I saw my cousin and people in his firm making tens, hundreds of thousands of dollars in a single day. What I failed to grasp was that those same people had big losing days, too. I was a more risk-averse person than some of these home-run hitters, and thus a more disciplined approach suited me better in the end. It can go both ways. Some people who try scalping find it too limiting and intense, instead preferring to come up with ideas and giving them room to play out. If you do not have any kids, do not build a five-bedroom house. If you hate the hustle and bustle of city life, build yourself a nice home in the suburbs. Develop a style that fits your personality and aligns with your goals as a trader or investor. Always be true to yourself.

The first two steps are vital to your long-term success, but they are only the beginning. Trading draws in a lot of people who have unrealistic expectations of immediate success. Profitability as a trader is not guaranteed and is definitely not guaranteed to come quickly. Just like building a house, building yourself up as a trader takes time. You must focus on execution on a smaller scale; you must pay attention to each detail, not just the sum of the parts.

Develop a style that fits your personality and aligns with your goals as a trader or investor.

At this point, you have built a strong foundation and you are confident the frame you have chosen suits you. Now, brick by brick, you must construct the substance of your house. Make sure each brick is laid correctly. Traders can achieve some early success, but if they are not trading in a way that is sustainable, the house will come crashing down. You must be able to repeat the process over and over again. If the pieces do come crashing down, you have to start small again. Trade by trade, brick by brick, day by day, you have to build yourself up. Each trade is a microcosm of a day, a week, a year. For each part, you must concentrate on executing properly and the result will take care of itself. If you become preoccupied with trying to "get rich quick" or burdened by losses, it becomes a vicious cycle. Nothing comes easy and few good things come quickly. Building a trading career is an arduous process.

Step-by-Step

To start the process, reduce each trade into its most basic parts. Especially for a short-term scalper, even the smallest misalignment can lead to failure. In the long-run, attention to detail is important for any kind of investor. When you experience losses or start to feel like you are losing control, just stop and tell yourself to take baby steps. Break down each step and things will again become clear.

First, evaluate your stock selection. Are you getting involved in the right trades, in the right stocks, at the right time? An important part of creating a successful strategy is understanding the circumstances that are conducive to good trades. Remind yourself what your perfect setup looks like and only get involved in those trades. In many cases, you may simply need to remind yourself that you know what you are doing. You have built the foundation and honed your strategy, now you just need to put it into practice.

Second, focus on your entries. The entry is the first part of a trade. When you are struggling, most of the time you will find you are being impatient. After a loss, it is natural to want to get it all back, but you must fight that tendency. Chasing trades will never get you anywhere. Be patient. If you miss a trade, it is not the worst thing in the world. Let the action come to you, and when that ideal setup presents itself, you will knock it

Be patient—chasing trades will never get you anywhere.

out of the park. My best period of the day was always the first hour. If I had a bad morning, I never chased trades in the afternoon to try to make money back because I knew that is not when I excel. Cleaning up your entries is the first step towards getting back on your feet. With a good entry, it is difficult for a trade to go against you.

Third, concentrate on the exit. You have identified a trade you like, made a clean entry, and now it is time to book profits. Make sure you get the most out of winners and that losers are minor events. In the beginning, do not be afraid to take trades quickly to generate positive cash flow and restore confidence. Do not hold trades against you. It is very simple if you let it be. For me, I would make a clean entry, identify a big bid in front, and aim for it. Boom—there is a positive trade. Good habits have now been formed and the positive trades stack up.

The final step in this process is like the final step in building a house. You have poured the foundation, you have put up the frame, and brick by brick you are building the house. Now it is time to decorate. Making a house into a home is all about adding your personal touch. Once you are seeing things clearly and executing both your entries and exits efficiently, start to be more aggressive. While it is important to get yourself back on track after a rough patch, being stagnant will hold you back. Being content to simply be positive will, over the long-term, hinder you from reaching your full potential. Add more size into your trades. If you really like a trade and momentum is there, maybe give it a little more room. When you are on, push it and get the most you can out of the market. When things start to slow down and you become less focused, get back to the basics.

WHEN THE GOING GETS TOUGH

Whenever you experience a devastating loss or go through a difficult period of trading, asking yourself the right questions is key to turning things around. Do not let your confidence be shaken. Over the years, I have trained so many traders who continue to come to me for advice when things are not going well. In a lot of cases, a simple dose of positivity does the trick. I remind them that they are good traders. I boil things down to the basics and they begin to see so clearly why they have been struggling. Usually, the impediment is not a slow market or a counter-intuitive move in a stock. The problem is usually that trader is getting in his own way. All traders will encounter many moments when they feel helpless, when they feel like giving up. I emphasize to them the quality that has allowed me to persevere through some trying times: staying positive. This is where you are and nothing is going to change that. You have a simple choice, stay and fight, or put your head down and sulk. Feeling sorry for yourself gets you nowhere. For some people, that may mean leaving the business, and there is nothing wrong with that. In fact, that is an important part of the evaluation process.

Pessimism is my least favorite quality in people. Life is filled with sadness, hurt, and grief. There is no avoiding the pain that comes with losing loved ones. There is no way of ducking the stress and anxiety that comes with finding your way both personally and professionally. It is easy to be a pessimist. It is easy to limp through life weighed down by our inadequacies, failures and losses. It is easy to expect little out of yourself and others.

I challenge you to shun the easy way. The people I admire most in the world are those who overcome handicaps and unusual challenges to achieve great things. These individuals choose to fight and choose to stay positive no matter how hard it is. The only way for you to reach your full potential as a trader or as a person is to come face to face with each loss. Accept things you cannot control and make an honest effort to improve everything you can. Pessimism will get you nowhere. Wake up every day with a renewed commitment to being the best version of you the person and you the trader. Day by day, you will become that person. Face every challenge head on, and at the end of the day, you will be content knowing you did your best.

● ● ●

Conclusion

||||||||||||||||||||||||||||||||||||||||||||||||||

T HE ONLY CONSTANT IN TRADING IS CHANGE. TRADES are like snowflakes, no two are exactly alike. In the same vein, no trading day is the same, and no market is the same. The evolution of the world financial markets has accelerated over the course of the last decade on a number of different levels. For one, we now live in a truly global economy. More important, though, are the many moving parts and high-stakes players that make fully understanding what is going on in the market nearly impossible. While confidence is a crucial ingredient for success in trading, humility is almost equally as important. The market is all-powerful, and anyone who thinks they have all the answers is a fool. To achieve market enlightenment, you must first resign yourself to the fact that you know nothing.

As time goes on and the market becomes more sophisticated and saturated, the value of humility becomes increasingly important. Trading as a career is becoming more difficult, and some long-time traders are being squeezed out of the business because they can not adapt. Black boxes and computers have come to dominate the tape, with the May 6, 2010 "Flash Crash" serving as a shocking revelation that anything is possible in today's volatile market. Computers are taking a growing slice of the profit pie and coming in to close competition with a large classification of short-term traders that previously enjoyed success scalping the Level II box. But you do not have to defeat the machines; this is not *Terminator 2*. You just have to fight for a different piece of the pie. While experienced traders may be reticent to abandon a strategy that has been their livelihood for the greater part of a decade, you have to know when to leave that old car on the side of the road.

It's a brave new world in the stock market, but it is far from impossible to make money and achieve your personal goals. Too often today we hear excuses. Many traders have a sense of entitlement. They feel like the market owes them something. The idea that the market *should* or *should not* behave in a certain way is as irrational as the market itself. The fact of the matter is, there is such a variety of factors that drive today's crowded market that it is foolish to think stocks will always (or ever) act in a rational way. The market is chaos, and that fact will only increase. The traders who will excel in the new era have accepted the difficult challenges that lie ahead, and put themselves in a position to succeed.

We want to leave you with some takeaways that describe more about what T3Live is, and why and how it was built to help traders prosper in the new era of the stock market.

WHY WE CREATED T3LIVE

Several years ago, in an effort to streamline strategy at our satellite offices, we set out to build a platform where we could communicate efficiently with remote traders. After implementing the first version of the website, we saw immediate results. Traders found incredible value in the education and analysis we were able to share on a daily basis, and as a result, they were able to become more dynamic and efficient. Communication is an important part of a trading floor, and we were able replicate that sense of teamwork in a virtual setting.

As we continued to improve and tweak this new platform, the fact that T3Live could be more than just a way for us to communicate with remote traders dawned on us. Realizing its potential as a retail product, we began to toy with the idea of opening up T3Live to a group of traders outside of the firm. The first beta version of the T3Live retail site was a huge hit, giving individual traders the chance to access the strategies of professional traders in real time. Trading is a difficult business, and trying to trade the increasingly complex markets alone, without the proper education and necessary guidance from experienced professionals, is a foolish proposition. With real-time access to experienced traders, however, anyone can learn how to trade like a pro.

From that point on, we have worked tirelessly to grow T3Live into a comprehensive resource for anyone who wants to learn how to make money as an active trader. T3Live is designed to empower the individual, to bridge the gap between Wall Street and Main Street. During a time of growing distrust between Wall Street firms and the American public, we are breaking down that cloak of secrecy by making T3Live the first fully transparent platform for traders. While T3Live has been in existence, the evolution of the stock market has accelerated. More so than ever before, it is important to manage the risks and opportunities associated with this dramatically altered landscape. The old ways of trading and investing no longer work, and it is harder than ever to be consistently profitable in the markets. T3Live allows its users to confront these changes head on.

PREPARATION IS KEY

When we created T3Live, we aimed to channel the most positive attributes of each of our top traders. During his long and successful career as an active trader, Scott Redler has distinguished himself in many areas, but most exceedingly in one: preparation.

Ten years ago, the need for thorough preparation was helpful, but not crucial. The structure of the stock market made it possible for the most talented traders to make money without even really trying. We all started our trading careers around the time of the tech boom, and it was a lucrative time to be a trader. Every day, there would be another hot tech stock that would skyrocket and make us hefty profits. All it took was a newswire and a trading account. Buy and watch the stock go higher. If you really wanted to, you could roll out of bed and into the office by 9:29 E.S.T. and, without any real preparation, make a killing.

For manual traders, the days of making money off small market inefficiencies are long gone. Structural changes and rapidly increasing high frequency trading (HFT) have ushered in a new era where only the strong survive.

The new era in the stock market necessitates a great deal of preparation, both on a short and long-term basis. You should be prepared for each year, each month, and, depending on your time frame, each day of your career as a trader or investor. Scott, for example, has been able to adapt to every market environment he has encountered because of his commitment to preparation. T3Live has a two-fold mission when it comes to preparation: giving you the fish, and teaching you how to fish. You will always make the most money on your own trades, but it never hurts to be pushed in the right direction from the start.

The Morning Gameplan

Scott prepares many of the pre-market materials available to T3Live subscribers. The Morning Gameplan price point sheet provides key price levels and notes for all of the most in-play stocks he follows on a daily basis. It is important as a manual trader to have a group of stocks you follow on a daily basis, and to become intimately familiar with price levels and action in those stocks. Your daily watch list can change based on stocks coming into and out of play, but there should always be a group that you know well.

The Morning Gameplan highlights minor and major support and resistance levels for Scott's current basket of stocks. Having a sense of price levels is extremely important in trading, as those are the levels where you will find the most volatility and explosive moves. Depending on whether you find yourself in a bull, bear, or sideways market cycle, you will treat those key levels differently, but having a mental picture of them is always crucial for your success.

While on the surface the Morning Gameplan provides subscribers with important levels to watch, we also hope it teaches traders how to build their own gameplan. Following another trader can only take you so far. At the end of the day, to have long-term success in the markets (or anything for that matter) you must be able to take ideas from inception to completion. You must be able to formulate trade ideas based on your own individual strategy. The Morning Gameplan provides a model for traders to learn how to build their own watch list. Whether it be screen-captured charts that are annotated, or a list of key price levels, having a routine and a game plan will allow you to develop that sense of feel that will allow you to excel as an active trader.

The Morning Call

In addition to the Morning Gameplan price point sheet, T3Live also provides live and on-demand pre-market videos for subscribers. In addition to his Morning Gameplan price point sheet, Scott films a Morning Call video where he goes over his daily analysis of the indices and his basket of stocks. He analyzes recent trends, notes upcoming announcements and provides actionable commentary for active traders. The price point sheet alone gives traders a great deal of information to use during the trading day, but the Morning Call video brings it all together. Scott goes over charts on screen, highlighting potential trade setups and pivot points. The combination of the Morning Gameplan sheet and the Morning Call video prepares each subscriber with a multitude of unique ideas for each and every trading day. In the process, that trader gains a valuable education that aids in the continuous learning process.

Master the Trade & Trades for Thought
Marc Sperling and Evan Lazarus also produce pre-market videos for T3Live, dubbed *Master the Trade* and *Trades for Thought,* respectively. In these videos, Marc and Evan outline, with defined trigger prices, targets, and stop-loss levels, their most compelling trade setups for that day. With their unique trading styles, they provide traders with another idea and perspective to watch during the trading day. Again, understanding the process they go through to formulate trade ideas is another valuable trading lesson each morning.

A commitment to preparation allows you to enter each trading day with the utmost confidence that you will make money. While you may not always be right with your ideas, you will greatly increase your efficiency and will be able to learn more quickly from your mistakes. T3Live provides you with both the resources and the education to build that confidence in yourself.

TRANSPARENCY IS THE ONLY WAY FORWARD
There are many trading blogs and websites out there today, but most lack the transparency to make them credible and effective. Active trading is not easy, and never will be again. Active traders are not always right, and any suggestion that they are is irresponsible. When we went about building T3Live, and as we continue to try to make it better each and every day, we want to make it, first and foremost,

highly transparent. The world of active trading is too often riddled these days with penny stock pump and dumper traders boasting consistent, riskless returns with their "groundbreaking" strategies. We aim to be a breath of fresh air for the Average Joe trader or investor who just wants the truth and some help achieving their personal financial goals through the market.

In terms of the economy, a lack of transparency is what got us into this mess in the first place. Over-leveraging and predatory lending built up a bubble that inevitably burst, and unfortunately, taxpayers ended up having to foot the bill. The point we are trying to make is that a shroud of deceit and secrecy gets nobody anywhere. As we mentioned previously, the public distrust for all things Wall Street is at an all-time high. People hear the term "trader" and immediately a negative picture comes to their mind. We like to consider ourselves the blue collar Wall Street. With T3Live, we have opened up our doors and our books to everyone, showing exactly what we are doing, when, and how we are doing it. The hope is that when we break down all delusions of grandeur, provide honest people with realistic expectations and professional analysis, we can create a value-added service that will help people improve their trading and themselves.

Virtual Trading Floor

The T3Live Virtual Trading Floor is the brain-child born from our desire to make the trading activities of our traders highly transparent. The Virtual Trading Floor includes a number of different elements, but the central features are live trader radios, live position windows, and the chat room.

Live Trader Radios

With live trader radios, we provide subscribers with real-time access to professional strategies and analysis. T3Live traders talk through all of their trades as they happen. Also, subscribers are granted a window into the mind of a successful professional trader. How does a profitable trader think? How does a daytrader execute short-term trades in the presence of black boxes and high-frequency trading? How does a longer-term investor use technical analysis to enter positions with the least risk possible? The live trader radios give the opportunity for anyone to learn directly from professional traders who have seen every type of market action.

Live Position Windows

The live position windows work in conjunction with the live trader radios, revealing all real positions that each trader is currently in. Symbols update in real time whenever any trader buys, sells, or short sells a security. T3Live traders are putting their money where their mouth is. There is no Monday morning quarterback or he-said-she-said; the records are there to prove how the trader actually executed his or her trades.

Chat Room

The chat room also functions in harmony with the rest of the tools on the Virtual Trading Floor. A physical trading floor should never be a one-way street, so neither should a virtual one. While education and analysis from professional traders is valuable, it is greatly enhanced when it becomes a two-way dialogue. The chat room, first and foremost, is a place for subscribers to interact with our professional traders. When they have a question about a trade or want input on an original idea, they can post directly to the chat and have their questions answered live. The radio feature makes it easy for T3Live's pro traders to provide in-depth feedback. The chat room istelf has also taken on a life its own as the subscriber base on T3Live.com has continued to grow. Currently, the T3Live chat room is home to a significant number of experienced and successful traders in their own right. As a stand-alone service, the chat room is an extremely valuable feature because it is full of insightful trade ideas and banter between subscribers. The Virtual Trading Floor has now become a truly expansive resource for traders to come together for a common goal while at the same time receiving guidance from seasoned pros.

As time goes on, the value of the Virtual Trading Floor will continue to increase. Every day, we are brainstorming features and changes to make the service more complete and value-added. With each passing day, our name becomes more visible and attracts a higher caliber of subscriber that adds value through the chat.

One thing is for sure, though. Transparency is the only way forward. By opening up our doors to anyone who wants to improve themselves, we hope to set an example for the trading world to follow. Information is power, and we hope to create a more intelligent and informed trading community by making our platform as transparent as possible.

EDUCATING YOURSELF AND MANAGING RISK

While education has always been valuable in trading, the evolution of the markets over the last decade has made a proper trading education dramatically more important. You can no longer get by doing things half-heartedly. You can't just "wing it." Many people have high expectations when they get into trading; they think everyone makes money in the market. The harsh reality is that uninformed people lose their shirt more often than not.

For an uneducated market participant, failure is a matter of "if," and not "when." We have had far too many conversations with opportunists who rush into the markets. The story is all too familiar. By the time a trader starts to get it, it is usually too late. Today's markets are too structured to take advantage of the unwitting trader, the fool who thinks they can learn on the job. The retrenchment of the trading industry over the last decade has ensured that most manual traders who trade large size are more sophisticated and knowledgeable than ever. High-frequency trading has dramatically increased risk for manual traders, but many still insist on entering the market before first truly learning about the implications of a highly computerized market.

Black boxes, or trading algorithms, are often programmed to take advantage of the irrational nature of the herd. Fear and greed are the two prevailing human emotions when it comes to money and the markets, and algorithms can quantify the conditions that produce those emotions. Key price levels become battlegrounds between high-speed trading 'bots, and the nature of support and resistance levels are vastly different than ever before. The only way to learn about these subtle but important changes is to constantly read, learn, study, and educate yourself.

We have a saying that we like to use when conveying the importance of risk management to newer traders: "Poor traders always think about how much they can make from a trade, but good traders always think about how much they stand to lose on a trade." When you phrase it that way, people tend to understand the point a little better. Given the implications of the new market, it is doubly important to tightly control risk. Risk management works on a trade by trade and more macro basis. As potential risks grow, you have to alter the type of trades you get involved in. Especially when you are a buyer, the "stairs up, elevator down" principle means you can stand to lose your shirt a lot more quickly than you grow your portfolio. Buy and hold investing may not be completely dead, but even investors need to understand how to enter long term positions with as little risk as possible. Risk management also needs to be undertaken on the basis of profit and loss. You must strictly adhere to daily, weekly, and monthly loss limits.

Immersion

The discussion of education and risk management brings me to my final point about the merits of T3Live. In addition to creating a symbiotic community where like-minded traders can interact and learn from experienced professionals, we encourage traders who are new to our forum to enroll in one of our education courses. While learning how to set stops and loss limits is important, the most important risk management tool you will ever own is an education.

Clean Slate

Over the years, we have gradually adjusted our training courses in order to provide the most benefit to as many people as possible. Currently, we have settled on a model in which we provide a two-day comprehensive crash course followed by a period of on-going practical application. In our two-day course, we like to wipe the slate clean of any preconceived notions, expectations, or biases. The first topic broached is the merits of active trading versus traditional modes of investing. We explain what active trading truly is, and how it has evolved over the years to become what it is today. It is hard to be a stock picker in the long-term even if you use the most earnest of fundamental investing principles. If you bought the Dow ten years ago, you will find yourself right back where you started, even a bit lower. During that time, however, active traders have taken cues from the market using technical analysis to make a career out of trading. The financial crisis of 2008 provided a perfect example of why you must have an active trading education to avoid not only financial hardship, but emotional strife as well! Many active traders had the best years of their career in 2008. We were flexible and nimble, and had the ability to, if nothing else, get into cash to avoid calamitous losses. While many saw retirement accounts dwindle to almost nothing, we were able to preserve capital and play both sides of the trade. While others were panicked and fearful, we were able to come in each day with level heads and make sound decisions.

Truly Active Trading

The next part of the course introduces the most important concepts in active trading. Candlestick charts are central to many of the risk management techniques employed by active traders. Each candlestick tells a powerful story about the tug of war between buyers and sellers, and understanding how to interpret candlesticks is the first step towards becoming a prudent active trader. The next major risk management tool we teach is time frame analysis, or the practice of looking at multiple chart time frames in order to find the least risky entry points for a trade. Using pivot points and trend analysis, you can develop a low-risk plan for each and every trade. The rest of the trading concepts portion of the course introduces you to other tools that we use to manage risk and identify trade setups. Moving averages, volume and slope analysis, support and resistance levels, retracements and extensions, and basic chart patterns are just a few examples of topics we cover in order to provide traders with additional tools.

Technical Analysis at Work

Many people have a misconception about technical analysis—that it only applies to daytraders and shorter-term swing traders. In today's market, that could not be any further from the truth. The methods of sound active trading, and technical analysis in general, can be applied on any time frame and incorporated into any type of investing strategy. The next section of the T3Live Active Trade Course delves into many specific, proprietary strategies we teach traders in order to help them craft an individual style and trading plan. Understanding proper entry bars can help you manage risk and maximize value on any type of trade. Rather than chasing moves or trying to fish bottoms, we teach you to use the various technical indicators in conjunction to get the best prices and the lowest levels of risk.

Advancements

After the strategies portion of the course, we cover a number of more advanced tools and analytics that can, once you have mastered the more basic principles, take your trading to the next level. Given the 24-hour news cycle and emerging importance of foreign markets, understanding how to interpret post-market gaps, for example, is vitally important for traders of all types. For short-term traders, understanding gaps is crucial to avoid chasing moves. For longer-term traders or investors, understanding the implications of certain types of gaps is paramount in order to avoid risky capital outlays. Relative strength and weakness is another topic covered in this course. While on the surface they are simple concepts, learning how to apply them in a real-life trading environment is a more difficult proposition. The T3Live Four-Tier System is another strategy covered in the Advanced Topics, and illustrates how a more nimble approach to trading and investing can even more greatly minimize risk and increase potential rewards. The section includes many more topics, and can evolve depending on what indicators are yielding success in any given market environment. Developing your own unique strategy that fits your personality is extremely important, and the advanced topics section arms you with tools and ideas to incorporate into your own plan.

New Market Psychology

The final day of the two-day course also includes a thorough discussion of the new market psychology. Market psychology has evolved in concert with the market itself, and more than ever, it is vitally important to understand. Just like in the advanced topics section, the nature of the market psychology portion of the course adjusts with the conditions in the market.

With the growing influence of black boxes and trading robots, the most important topic covered today in the market psychology portion of the course is how you should adjust strategy based on the action you see around you. Many of the old methods and ways of thinking are outdated. You must be able to ignore the white noise of the market that is computer manipulation and focus only on the things you can control.

In this section of the course, we will always discuss the personal barriers that prevent some traders from ultimately having success and becoming consistently profitable. To be a good trader or investor, you must know yourself well and avoid letting emotions get the best of you. You must avoid becoming a perfectionist and learn to manage expectations depending on market environment. You need to acquire the tools to get out of a slump and avoid heavy losses when you are not "on." Perhaps most importantly, you must learn the power of a positive mindset. Nadav embodies the results of a positive mindset, which is likely why he has enjoyed so much success as a trainer for new traders. The market will always evolve; trading is cyclical and good times will come and go. The one thing that must remain constant amid all the turmoil is your resolve. While it is important to recognize when it is time to move on from trading or overhaul your approach to the market, there will always be a way for you to achieve your personal expectations in the market.

Comprehensive Trading Plan

In the final piece of the course, we help the trader put it all together with a comprehensive trading plan. Before making your first trade, you should always outline your goals, expectations, and strategy. Each trader at T3Live has developed a plan that defines their trading and dictates their level of success. You are only as good as your plan and strategy. It is easy to get lost and turned around in today's crowded market, and the value of a detailed plan has grown exponentially. During this portion of the course, we bring in highly experienced traders to share examples of their own trading plans and guide you in your personal journey.

Continuing Education

After the two-day course, traders are armed with an education that will serve them well in trading the market. Learning the concepts and strategies is only half the battle, however, and we encourage traders to continue with T3Live for our Active Trading Lab. No matter where you choose to seek a trading education, it is important to have professional guidance throughout your development, and especially during the early stages. During the Active Trading Lab, graduates of the Active Trading Course have the opportunity to trade alongside professional traders as they further their education in a real market setting. Traders have the option of training in our Manhattan trading headquarters or virtually online through our revolutionary Virtual Training Room.

The Virtual Training Room is similar to the Virtual Trading Floor on T3Live.com, but provides a much greater degree of education. The enrollees in the lab have the opportunity to watch the instructors' screens as they demonstrate each of the techniques and concepts covered in the course. While watching traders apply strategies in real time, there is the opportunity for questions and discussion. In addition, each member of the lab has the option of having their own trading plan and actual trades reviewed. In trading, learning is doing, and education is an on-going journey. Many of the most powerful lessons you learn will come during painful losses or well-executed trades, and it is crucial that when you start to get out of your comfort zone, you have the attention of an experienced professional to point you in the right direction.

Getting Personal

In addition, we craft individual coaching plans for traders who want to further their education on an even more personal level. T3Live educators make time during and after the trading day to help others shrink the learning curve. The goal is to provide any individual with the education options he or she needs in order to become a successful active trader.

The value of education, and in turn, risk management, has grown tremendously in the last decade. At T3Live, we have worked tirelessly to build a platform where anyone in the world can come to learn about active trading. While we have become adept at training new traders, we are not just professional teachers; we are in the markets every single day. We are going through the journey alongside you and understand the challenges as they present themselves. The market is changing at a rapid pace, and you must have the wherewithal to keep up.

FROM SEAN: THE FINAL WORD

Everyone, over the journey of their life, comes to a point when they must decide how they will manage their wealth. Each individual, depending on their personality, time, resources, and goals, must define their plan for growing their wealth or planning for retirement. Money is not a be-all-end-all in life, but it can be a tool to provide security and happiness for yourself and your family. Money can often inspire the most extreme of human emotions. Greed, fear, despair, exuberance. Over the course of my career, and the careers of my partners at T3, we have certainly run the gamut of human emotions when it comes to money. Over the course of the last decade, since the grand illusion which was the tech boom, we all were forced to come to grips with what it means to make and lose money.

The most powerful feeling I ever felt, and I am sure Marc, Scott, Nadav and Evan would agree, was the feeling that I was in control. When I finally learned to harness the power of active trading, it set me free. Active trading can be defined in many ways, but first and foremost it is simply a plan for managing money and hopefully achieving your personal financial goals. I fell in love with the markets and made trading my career. I have employed a number of different strategies successfully, and continue to push the envelope to stay ahead of the curve. Each person must define their level of commitment to the market and build a plan to match.

The goal when we created T3Live was to provide individuals with both the education and on-going guidance necessary to achieve their personal goals. Each service we offer at T3Live. com is designed to help you on the path to seizing control.

With education services, we hope to inform people about the risks of the new market and teach them how to regain control. Through daily market analysis and trade ideas, we hope to arm people with actionable ideas and commentary. On the Virtual Trading Floor, we aim to cultivate a community where anyone can come to learn from experienced professionals while also sharing the journey with other like-minded individuals. The synergies achieved through the Virtual Trading Floor continue to grow each and every day as more traders learn about T3Live.com.

We hope our life stories and trading lessons help you put together the pieces of the puzzle. Not everyone is cut out to be a daytrader. Not everyone is cut out to be an entrepreneur. We all have different personalities, goals, and expectations. But no matter your place in life, active trading can arm you with powerful tools to take control.

Epilogue

TRANSPARENCY UNDERLIES EVERYTHING WE DO IN THE financial markets. It's been 3 years since I jumped on the 4 train for the first day of my internship with T3 Live and a lot has changed. The Partners are still all thriving and working together as a team to grow T3 as a whole. They have also evolved with the changing markets and the regulatory landscape. Ponzi schemes and insider trading have frequented the headlines for the past several years and the financial industry has not fared well. During a time of great scrutiny when many firms are looking for new ways to step out of the public eye, T3 has gone in the other direction and has become a Registered SEC Broker-dealer and Member of the CBOE Stock Exchange (CBSX) under the name T3 Trading Group, LLC (www.T3Trading.com).

T3 Trading Group, LLC and T3 Live, LLC are affiliated, but separate companies. All trading is done on a Proprietary basis through T3 Trading Group, LLC and T3 Live is an online financial media network and education platform that provides active traders and investors with market analysis, real-time access to strategies, and in-depth training from real-traders, in real-time.

Becoming a regulated entity is not without its challenges, but it has meant even more transparency and structure for the T3 community. Change is good and necessary. The Partners of T3 have shown me this first hand, and as the T3 companies continue to grow I look forward to seeing how the next chapter unfolds.

About The Authors

||||||||||||||||||||||||||||||||||||||||||||||||||||||||||||||||||||||||||

SEAN HENDELMAN ⊢────────────────────────────────o
is the Co-Founder and Chief Executive Officer of T3 Live and
a partner in T3 Trading Group, LLC. He oversees all operations and directs the vision of the company. Mr. Hendelman
specializes in high-frequency automated trading.

Experience
Mr. Hendelman has been in the equity trading industry for
more than ten years. He began his career in 1997 at Greenwich
Capital Markets where he became Vice-President focusing on
sales and trading information technology before moving
on to satisfy his passion for entrepreneurship. In 1999, he
became a partner and equity trader for a proprietary trading firm before opening his own statistical arbitrage hedge
fund, Pulsar Capital Management, LLC. Several years later,

Mr. Hendelman formed Nexis Capital, LLC in 2005. While managing Nexis, Mr. Hendelman expanded to the algorithmic trading field through WB Capital, LLC, where he became a highly profitable black box trader. The T3 Live education service was created after the merger between Nexis Capital and Sperling Enterprises, LLC.

Education

Mr. Hendelman received an M.B.A. in Management / Entrepreneurship and Marketing from the NYU Stern School of Business and graduated with honors with a B.A. in Economics from the University of Michigan.

MARC SPERLING

is the co-founder and President of T3 Live and a partner in T3 Trading Group LLC.

Experience

Mr. Sperling has been actively trading for more than ten years, and has been successful in trading since the beginning of the dot-com boom. After gaining notoriety for his success as a broker at Olde Discount Brokers in 1996, he left the firm to pursue his own goals as a trader. After several years as a trader at Broadway Trading, in 2000 Mr. Sperling started his own firm, Sperling Enterprises, LLC. Under his direction, in 2007, Sperling Enterprises merged with Nexis Capital and T3 Live was created soon thereafter.

Education

Marc received a B.S. in Marketing from Ithaca College.

NADAV SAPEIKA

is the Chief Operating Officer of T3 Live and a partner in T3 Trading Group LLC. He manages business operations, business development, and oversees the company's technology infrastructure.

Experience

After several years as a short-term trader and trainer, Mr. Sapeika became a partner at Nexis Capital, LLC with Sean Hendelman. In 2007, Mr. Sapeika helped facilitate the merger between Nexis Capital and Sperling Enterprises to create T3 Capital Management, LLC, and ultimately T3 Live, a separate entity, was born. T3 Capital Management in 2010 transitioned into a broker-dealer, T3 Trading Group, LLC.

Education

Mr. Sapeika received a J.D. from Rutgers School of Law and graduated with a B.A. in Economics and Rabbinic Studies from Yeshiva University.

SCOTT REDLER

is the Chief Strategic Officer of T3 Live and a partner in T3 Trading Group, LLC. He develops all trading strategies for the service and acts as the face of T3 Live. Mr. Redler focuses on thorough preparation and discipline as a trader.

Experience

Mr. Redler has been trading equities for more than ten years and has more recently received widespread recognition from the financial community for his insightful, pragmatic approach. He began his career as a broker and venture capitalist where he was able to facilitate relationships that led him into trading. Beginning his trading career at Broadway Trading in 1999, Mr. Redler moved on with Marc Sperling to Sperling Enterprises, LLC after establishing himself as one of the best young traders in the firm. As a manager at Sperling Enterprises, he continued to trade actively while working closely with all traders in the firm to dramatically increase performance.

Mr. Redler has participated in more than 30 triathlons and one IronMan competition, exhibiting a work ethic that also defines his trading. His vast knowledge and meticulous attention to detail has led to regular appearances on CNBC, Fox Business, Bloomberg, and he is a regular contributor to Minyanville and Forbes' Intelligent Investing blog. He has been quoted in the *Wall Street Journal* and *Investor's Business Daily*, among other publications. Mr. Redler produces much of the media and content available to subscribers and followers on T3Live.

Education
Scott received a B.B.A. in Marketing/Finance from the State University of New York at Albany, graduating Magna Cum Laude from Albany's School of Business.

EVAN LAZARUS
is the Chief Knowledge Officer of T3 Live and a partner in T3 Trading Group, LLC. He leads the company's strategic vision for trader education and manages all of T3 Live's intellec-

tual property. Mr. Lazarus employs a technical swing trading strategy.

Experience

Mr. Lazarus has been in the equity trading business for 11 years. After three years at Freelance Equity Trading, LLC, he took a managing director position at Sperling Enterprises, LLC. At Sperling Enterprises, Mr. Lazarus, along with Scott Redler, managed the firm's traders and developed its training program. His core competency lies in understanding the difficult psychological aspect of trading, and his ability to mentor other traders. Mr. Lazarus became a partner in Sperling Enterprises in 2006 and stepped into the role of Chief Operating Officer for the company. In 2007, he helped facilitate the creation of T3 Capital Management, which in 2010 transitioned into a broker-dealer, T3 Trading Group, LLC. Mr. Lazarus now manages all training content at T3 Live.

Education

Mr. Lazarus received a B.A. in Communications from the University of Miami.

B

Marketplace Books is the preeminent publisher of trading, investing, and finance educational material. We produce professional books, DVDs, courses, and electronic books (ebooks) that showcase the exceptional talent working in the investment world today. Started in 1993, Marketplace Books grew out of the realization that mainstream publishers were not meeting the demand of the trading and investment community. Capitalizing on the access we had through our distribution partner Traders' Library, Marketplace Books was launched, and today publishes the top authors in the industry — household names like Jack Schwager, Oliver Velez, Larry McMillan, Sheldon Natenberg, Jim Bittman, Martin Pring, and Jeff Cooper are just the beginning. We are actively acquiring some of the brightest new minds in the industry including technician Jeff Greenblatt and programmers Jean Folger and Lee Leibfarth.

From the beginning student to the professional trader, our goal is to continually provide the highest quality resources for those who want an active role in the world of finance. Our products focus on strategic information and cutting edge research to give our readers the best education possible. We are at the forefront of digital publishing and are actively pursuing innovative ways to deliver content. At our Traders' Forum events, our readers get the chance to learn and mingle with our top authors in a way unprecedented in the industry. Our titles have been translated in most major world languages and can be shipped all over the globe thanks to our preferred online bookstore, TradersLibrary.com.

Visit us today at:

www.marketplacebooks.com & www.traderslibrary.com

CPSIA information can be obtained
at www.ICGtesting.com
Printed in the USA
BVHW071913160920
588925BV00003B/251/J

9 781592 804498